Sun Valley

A Biography

Sun Valley

A Biography

Doug Oppenheimer & Jim Poore

Beatty Books · Boise, Idaho

To Jane & Arthur Oppenheimer and Beryl & Merrill Poore.

ISBN 0-916238-04-0, cloth
ISBN 0-916238-02-4, paper
Library of Congress Catalog Card Number: 76-27-113
R. O. Beatty & Associates, P.O. Box 763, Boise, Idaho 83702
Copyright © 1976 by R. O. Beatty & Associates
All rights reserved
Printed in the United States of America

Contents

In 1935, as Chairman of the Board of the Union Pacific Railroad, I had been working to strengthen the image of the railroad as a constructive force in the depression years in the west for the development of industry and passenger travel. In my travels to Europe as a banker, I had learned of the great popularity of their ski resorts. At that time the United States had only limited skiing, and I thought we might make an asset out of the liability of having so much snow along our route. In addition, ski resorts might become a much-needed new industry in the mountain states.

I employed Count Felix Schaffgotsch, a friend of mine who was well versed in European winter resorts, to search for the ideal area for a similar American resort.

I received from Felix discouraging reports week after week from his explorations. Finally in mid-February I got a message: "I've found it! Come and see for yourself!" What he'd found was glorious—powder snow over open slopes, with Bald Mountain close at hand. By unanimous agreement the place was called Sun Valley. It named itself.

Events happened in rapid succession. With the approval of the UP Board of Directors, construction started in May, and the lodge was opened for Christmas that year, 1936. It had so much publicity that it was already called the "St. Moritz of America" in the press. The first chair lifts in the world, invented by Union Pacific engineers, were built by the American Bridge Company in time for the opening. Austrian ski instruc-

Foreword

tors were imported to found the Sun Valley Ski School. Challenger Inn, designed as an Austrian mountain village, followed the next year. Instead of the European type of funicular from bottom to top, we developed the three-phase chairlift, which added greatly to the versatility of skiing on extraordinary Bald Mountain.

I congratulate Mr. Bill Janss for the splendid manner in which he has developed the mountain with additional ski lifts and ingenious equipment to keep the runs in good shape. Sun Valley has become a delightful summer vacation area as well. Now Mr. Janss has greatly enlarged the facilities with the attractive groups of condominiums.

Sun Valley achieved its objective of encouraging the development of ski resorts in many parts of the west, and Idaho has the pioneer resort it is justly proud of. My hopes have come true.

This book tells the story of Sun Valley and the people involved in it in fascinating detail, and the authors have captured, in words and rare photographs, the special feeling of the place. I hope you enjoy reading about Sun Valley as much as we enjoyed creating it.

W. AVERELL HARRIMAN

Washington, D.C.
May, 1976

Sun Valley is an American fantasy, of sun-tanned gods and goddesses, of wild parties, of skiers flashing through deep powder under a blinding sun, of nights in front of a crackling fire—of a world apart, where your other life spins and whirls away from you. Sun Valley stands alone historically as an elegant example of American inventiveness. While it may be all the things people dream it to be, it is also very real, and its story is one of discovery, imagination, and innovative engineering. The beautiful people come and go, but Sun Valley endures, because of the people who built it and who maintain it. What we have tried to do is rediscover the mixture of foresight, ingenuity, and audacity that has enabled Sun Valley to last through the years. Originally a "manufactured product" perhaps, it has since evolved naturally, with a compelling influence of its own that transcends publicity photos and press releases. That mystique above all is what we've attempted to convey in these pages.

Preface

The Authors

Wood River

It was not a time for adventure. Families needed to be fed and a dollar was a rare possession. The Great Depression, signaled by the stock market collapse in 1929, was still strangling the American economy in the early thirties. Parties once raged on Park Avenue; fat businesses fed on the prosperity of the twenties; and America's golden lustre twinkled and glittered in the eyes of the world's masses, who longed to be a part of it. By 1932, however, a square meal and an hour's work had come to mean "the good life" in the United States.

When newspapers were flapped open each morning, news of a world in chaos tumbled out. In 1932, World War I veterans marched on Washington, demanding that Congress pay their promised bonuses in full. Washington turned a deaf ear and set loose a pack of young soldiers to sweep the veterans out of sight and send them home without their money. In 1933, Adolph Hitler became German Chancellor. The nations of the world, already numbed by pressing financial problems, were introduced to the man who eventually would lead them to the final depression-breaker: World War II. That same year, Franklin D. Roosevelt said all banks must be closed. The only "good news" was that prohibition in America ended in 1933, and so now the once-rich and the always-poor could drown their sorrows legally. In Germany in 1934, the offices of President and Chancellor were consolidated and, chillingly, Hitler became the *Fuehrer*.

By 1935, America was six years past the start of the depression and four years from the ominous rumblings

When a Nickel was a Fortune

. . . the Question of Why

of World War II. The everyday life of most Americans seemed to be growing better. Programs were underway to ensure employment, and children were going to bed on half-filled instead of empty stomachs. The depression and its effects, however, still hung in the air like forbidding storm clouds.

At a time like this, who could be thinking of skiing? When most of the nation was standing in bread lines, who'd want to worry about lift lines? Families used to filling their plates with potatoes from home-grown gardens, fishing to the bottom of a well-worn change purse to find a penny for a treat for the children, didn't have the time or the inclination to look for the "perfect powder."

There were, however, men who did. The depression didn't keep everyone down. In the effort to escape the black mood of their Spartan life-style, people still lined up in front of the movie theaters to see the newest Mary Pickford, Errol Flynn, or Frederic March movie.

People were still listening to the radio, making rich men out of Jack Benny, George Burns, Eddie Cantor, and Bob Hope.

And the trains were still running, which meant William Averell Harriman still had a job and the power and influence to do just about anything he wanted.

Averell's father, Edward Henry Harriman, had taken control of the bankrupt Union Pacific Railroad in 1897 and built it into a giant of the transportation industry. If America was going to be brought to its knees, that day would start when the Union Pacific's tracks, symbolic

Ski touring

12

of the nation's expansion, rusted into disuse. But Averell Harriman and Union Pacific were far from the rust stage in 1935. Instead, Harriman was vigorous in his outlook of America's and Union Pacific's future, and went about showing what could be done in hard times.

Edward Henry Harriman had insisted that his son climb through the ranks of Union Pacific. Averell started when he was seventeen years old, working the railroad, traversing the West, sweating in the steaming sun with the company's hired hands. All in all, he gained a healthy respect for the vastness of the land the U.P. served. He went on to graduate from Yale. By 1935 he had become chairman of the board of Union Pacific. And by 1935, Averell Harriman had decided that, depression or no depression, the time was right for an American ski resort.

Today Harriman takes the stance that in 1935 America was coming out of the depression. The worst years were over, he points out, and there was a need for optimism.

"The very fact that it was a depression is one of the reasons we wanted to do this," said Harriman. "There was enough money by that time. There was still a lot of unemployment but there was an improvement in business. In 1936 and 1937 there was a slight recession again, but it was generally improved with the stock market."

Skiing 1935-style in America was largely confined to the icy trails of New England, where sub-zero temperatures and gloomy skies made the sport hard to promote.

William Averell Harriman

There were no real mountains. The 1932 Winter Olympics had been held in Lake Placid, New York, but it was still a far cry from the classy winter playgrounds of France, Austria, and Germany.

Don Fraser remembers Lake Placid with a shudder.

"It was a winter resort and they had bobsledding and ice-skating and curling," said Fraser. "And they had a little skiing. But they had no mountains there, really,

Early slalom race, skier Dick Durrance

that were worthy at that time of the ski jump. There was nothing, really, in the way of downhill skiing."

Most Americans saw little excitement in the sport. Fraser, a member of the U.S. Winter Olympics team (his wife Gretchen later was the first American to win a gold medal, at St. Moritz in 1948), had to live with that apathy. The 1936 games were held in Germany's storybook setting in the Alps at Garmisch. Fraser had to work his way over on a fruit boat, "a Norwegian freight-

er," he recalled. The trip took thirty-one days and gave him plenty of time, between work shifts, to sand and polish his precious skis.

And skis were indeed precious in 1936. To make sure he had the best possible, Fraser made his own. "It was about the only way you could get a pair of skis that you wanted in those days," he said. "We lived along the west coast [in Vancouver, Washington] and there were skis available in the East, like Gregg and North-

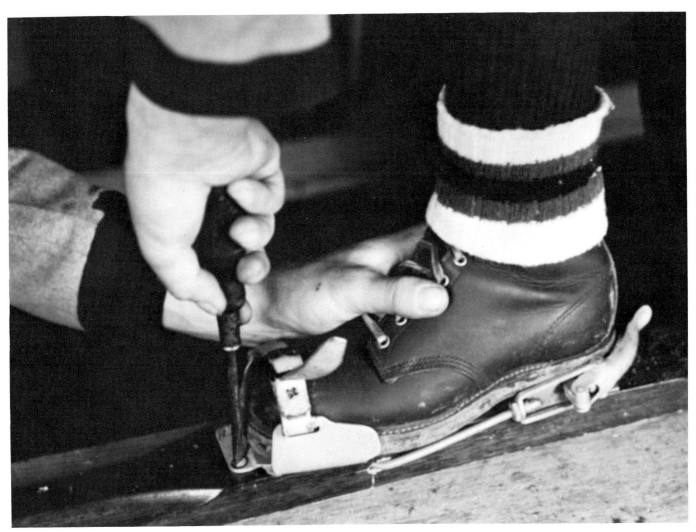

Fitting early ski boot into binding

land. But they were expensive and they weren't very good, really, except for the jumping skis. And there were no cross-country skis at all then. You had to make your own cross-country skis. I made mine out of birch; they were beautiful."

Fraser made it to Germany but on a practice run hit a tree and, "I was sidelined completely."

If Sammy Baugh or Y.A. Tittle or Joe Namath lay twisting in pain on the ground from a brutal hit by a defensive lineman, America would wince with regret.

If anybody noticed when Don Fraser rammed the tree, it was probably only a few of the friends he'd made on the Norwegian freighter. America, then, was not exactly crazy about skiing in 1936.

Interviewed in 1976, forty years after Fraser crashed in the German Alps, Averell Harriman nodded and smiled at the lack of interest in skiing back then. "I can't say that it was almost unknown, but it was a very limited sport," Harriman explained. "There was a certain amount of skiing in the East and a certain amount in the West, but it was limited to a relatively tiny group of people. It's rather hard to realize that it was utterly an unknown sport to the average public, and now, of course, it's one of the most popular in the country."

To find the proper place to ski in 1936, you had to search for it; distances were greater because transportation was slower, and it was almost impossible to find a decent ski area within reasonable driving distance. "And the skiing was not very good," Harriman continued, "because the runs were rather narrow, and they were rather icy in the East. There was no major ski resort anywhere in the West. We were the first to build one."

Although it didn't have to be an expensive sport—an enthusiast of moderate means could, like Don Fraser, make his own skis; and even manufactured equipment was not so costly then—skiing was still a little exclusive in the 1930's. Like polo, it was something the average person just didn't do. Accessibility seemed to be the key.

The real resorts, the glittering diamonds of skiing, were in Europe, especially in the mountainous countries at its core: Davos, San Anton, Kitzbühel, St. Moritz, Murren—largely a collection of jumbled letters to most Americans in the thirties, but skiing-heaven to Europeans and the few Americans who crossed the Atlantic to enjoy their endless snowfields.

Harriman discovered this while traveling the trail of international finance, an area he was as adept in as he was at running a railroad. As an international banker, Harriman had often visited his European—and even New York—colleagues only to find empty offices and messages that any further business would have to be conducted in some snowy wilderness, if it was to be pursued at all.

"That's where my idea came from, because I went abroad in the winter to see my friends and discovered that even my rather rotund German friends, less-than-slim German bankers, used to take a couple of weeks off in the winter for a vacation," said Harriman. "Rather

Skiers in high mountain country

than take off in the summer, they wanted to go and ski. So I looked into it."

Harriman, sparrow thin and very athletic all his life, sensed he—and America—was missing something. On one of those trips, Harriman decided that the Union Pacific could do something about that.

Union Pacific had always been a leader in rail transportation, putting the first streamliner on the tracks in 1933. Such a bold move at such a time, when money for travel was tight, naturally brought the railroad banner headlines. Once again, Harriman insists that the depression was not a major issue, citing an expression used in the twenties to make his point: "Throw him out—he's breaking my heart." Harriman heard it used in the business community and, closer to his own heart, in the railroad industry. Every time a railroad president got into trouble, Harriman said, he'd whine about "what a terrible poor deal the railroads were getting." The answer they got, explained Harriman, was "Nobody is going to be interested in you if you wail about yourselves. You've got to be doing something for the people."

Harriman agreed. And so began the drive to improve Union Pacific's image. "We were working out of the depression at the time, and the streamlined train was the thing." The fleet of trains grew and the coaches were improved. Reclining seats were added and inexpensive meals were introduced.

"One of the things that everybody objected to was the fact that the train crews were so disagreeable to the passengers, which was true," said Harriman. "So we advertised how polite the Union Pacific train crews were, and the crews took it up. If you advertise that a man is polite, he's got to be polite." In another move to attract travelers, Union Pacific put stewardesses on its

Sun Valley country

18

coaches, the forerunner of a service airline passengers take for granted today.

And passenger service did grow. But still, it was not enough. Visions of the empty bankers' chairs in Munich and Bonn flashed through Harriman's mind.

The Santa Fe Railroad, one of Union Pacific's chief competitors, had an advertising slogan, "Go to the Sun Through the Sun." That made sense. If a potential passenger in New York City wanted to reach Los Angeles, a railroad timetable calling for a lazy swing through sunshiny Arizona and New Mexico would catch his eye.

It made sense for the Santa Fe. But it didn't make sense for the Union Pacific, which was saddled with deep-freeze runs through Colorado, Utah, Wyoming, and Idaho during the winter. What did make sense to Harriman was to take that cold and make it pay.

"I looked into the question of skiing vacations and discovered that they were very popular in Europe," Harriman said. "And I thought we'd make an asset out of a liability—in other words, the snow. And the more I thought of it, the more I thought we could start a new industry in the West."

Averell Harriman was born in New York City, and throughout his long political career—Governor of New York, Secretary of Commerce, Ambassador to Russia, and chief negotiator in the Vietnam-Paris peace talks in the late sixties—he has appeared to be very much the sophisticated easterner. Still he has for a long time had very strong feelings for the rugged simplicity of the American West.

Idaho has been a part of Averell Harriman's life since 1909, when he first visited the state as a worker on the Union Pacific. His father had purchased a giant tract of land in Idaho in the early 1900's, eventually called the Railroad Ranch. Averell and his brother, E. Roland Harriman, a New York investment banker, still own it. The land, 14,000 acres of wilderness in southeastern Idaho, has been willed to the Idaho Park Foundation for a future state park.

But long before Railroad Ranch became a gift of goodwill from the Harriman family to Idaho, Averell Harriman claims he was thinking about doing something to help the state. That, and to help improve Union Pacific's Rocky Mountain passenger service. "We'd built some hotels on the north rim of the Grand Canyon," said Harriman, "but we'd done nothing for Idaho. We had a monopoly on rail transportation in Idaho."

A monopoly on rail transportation in Idaho and, at the same time, a monopoly on an idea. Whether that idea sprang from a desire to help population-scarce Idaho develop a smattering of industry, or to improve Union Pacific's passenger service in the West, or to bring skiing to America in the finest European tradition isn't important. What is important is that the idea took hold, and sleepy Idaho was to be thrust suddenly into national prominence—a place where Hollywood stars and Greek shipping tycoons would gather to ski, party, and leave behind money and legends.

The country was about to be handed Sun Valley.

Early Ketchum

Averell Harriman had his idea and he had the massive facilities of the Union Pacific Railroad at his disposal. But that wasn't enough. Averell Harriman had no idea where to build his ski resort. It would be costly to send out an expedition of inexperienced Americans to select the site, build the resort, and then have blizzards, bad snow, or freezing temperatures kill it.

One of Harriman's big problems was that he couldn't tackle the job by himself. He was not very familiar with skiing.

"I had skied as a boy at school—you know, where you put your foot into a loop and slide down hills," said Harriman. "But I'd never done any real skiing before Sun Valley."

To carry out his plans, then, and find a place in America where a ski resort better than the finest the Swiss or French had to offer could be built, Harriman needed somebody who was a combination skier, visionary, tour guide, outdoorsman, and pathfinder. He needed a man who could find the best piece of land for the purpose and imagine it dressed up with ski lodges, runs, ice rink, and whatever else the resort was to offer.

He turned to Count Felix Schaffgotsch.

Schaffgotsch was an Austrian who had a habit of turning up in European society. Harriman isn't sure where he first met the count, but he knew the name from his business contacts abroad. Schaffgotsch was a dashing young bachelor in his early thirties who knew something about European ski resorts. As a result, Harriman sought Schaffgotsch's counsel on Sun Valley.

Searching for the Perfect Place

. . . the Count's Decision

"He was not an outstanding skier, but he was experienced in handling tourists," said Harriman. "He knew what people wanted and he knew all *about* skiing."

Harriman brought Schaffgotsch to the United States in the autumn of 1935 and gave him a simple set of instructions—scour the American West and find an area where the powder was dry, where the sun shone all day, and where the harsh winds of winter didn't penetrate. "I told him to go all over and pick the place he would recommend," Harriman recalled.

There was just one catch—Harriman preferred that place be somewhere on the Union Pacific line. So it wasn't exactly as if the foreign count was shoved out the door of Harriman's New York office to wander a strange land without the slightest idea of where he was going. "You see," explained Harriman, "the railroad organization took hold of him and steered him around; so he wasn't on a Lewis and Clark expedition. He had the Union Pacific to help him."

Schaffgotsch took the assignment and headed west, the perfect picture of a European aristocrat in search of a ski resort. The pencil-thin Austrian went out dressed in flannel knickers, a bulky-knit sweater, woolen knee socks, and a waist-length, double-breasted windbreaker. To cover his slowly receding hairline, he wore an alpine hat.

The count visited areas that have become legendary in American ski circles—Aspen, Jackson Hole, Alta, Lake Tahoe. And in every one of them, he found something wrong.

Visiting Yosemite in California, Schaffgotsch was pelted by blizzards, and in the comfort of his hotel room he scratched that from his list. An area prone to blizzards would send people scurrying to their rooms, and soon the word would spread that the skiing was bad.

Schaffgotsch went to Aspen and, after wandering its pine-choked slopes and sampling the skiing, said no. Aspen, Schaffgotsch declared, was too high. "He said his idea was—and I confirmed this in Europe—that a ski resort shouldn't be over 6,000 feet, because it affects too many people," said Harriman.

Besides, Aspen was not on the Union Pacific's line.

Schaffgotsch journeyed to Alta, Utah. He liked the skiing there, but said it was too near Salt Lake City. If they decided on Alta, he reported, the area would be overrun by weekend skiers and the detached atmosphere of a ski resort would be lost.

What Schaffgotsch wanted was a destination ski resort, one that would give the feeling of alpine seclusion.

With his alternatives dwindling, Schaffgotsch left for Idaho. He reached Boise, then a slow-moving little town of just over 25,000, in January of 1936, and was assigned U.P.'s area representative, William J. Hynes, to help him on his search. Hynes, special agent in charge of freight and passenger service, was a former state legislator, a well-known man about Boise, and, for Harriman and Schaffgotsch, the ultimate pathfinder.

"I didn't know a damn thing about what the hell a ski resort was, to tell you the truth," Hynes now admits. "I kind of thought it was a waste of time and money. I didn't believe U.P. was really even interested in it."

But U.P. was, and told Hynes that he was to escort Schaffgotsch anywhere he wanted to go, anywhere there might be a chance of finding the place he sought. So, doubts still lingering in his mind, the forty-six-year-old Hynes traveled to Pocatello in Southeastern Idaho to meet this European count the Union Pacific wanted him to shepherd around Idaho or, if need be, across the borders into neighboring states.

Immediately they moved away from Idaho to Wyoming. With Hynes by his side, and bundled warmly against the elements, Schaffgotsch rode a sleigh through Teton Pass to look at Jackson Hole. What he saw was beautiful country, mountains with all the potential for a good ski industry. But Jackson Hole, though destined to become one of America's best-known ski resorts, had flaws in Schaffgotsch's eyes.

"It was kind of a hard place to get into," Hynes explained. Schaffgotsch wanted the Wyoming State government to guarantee they would keep the road open from Victor to Jackson Hole. "They said no, they'd bring the people in from Rock Springs." Unfortunately, Rock Springs was 185 miles from Jackson Hole, and in the winter—especially Wyoming's chilling, wind-battering winters—the trip to Jackson Hole would have been too much of a hardship. While a ski fanatic might have made the trip once, it's doubtful even he would have braved the road from Rock Springs—the closest Union Pacific dropoff point—to Jackson Hole a second time.

Count Felix Schaffgotsch

23

And then there were the trees—too many trees in Schaffgotsch's view. They would clog and destroy the atmosphere he was searching for. Jackson Hole was crossed off the list.

The next stop was Spencer, Idaho, a small, quiet town on the Montana border. Spencer seemed ideal. It was surrounded by vast snowfields, wide open, with acres of treeless hills. But something wasn't right to Schaffgotsch, who turned his noble nose in the air and marched away. Hynes never knew why Schaffgotsch rejected Spencer—perhaps because it was too remote even for him.

The search seemed dead-ended. Schaffgotch had been to California, Oregon, Utah, Wyoming and Colorado, and after six weeks knew no more where Harriman's resort might one day rest than he did when he started. Days of traveling, by car, dog sled, sleigh, plane, and of course train, seemed to have dulled the count's keenness for the hunt. One day Schaffgotsch looked at Hynes, shook his hand warmly, and in his meticulous English said he was bringing his Idaho search to an end. There was a place in Colorado he would look at once more, and if it didn't seem any better the second time than it had the first, he would head back to New York City to face Averell Harriman with the unhappy news that there was no St. Moritz, no Kitzbühel, hidden in the American West.

Before he boarded the train, almost as an afterthought, Schaffgotsch said, "If you find anything, let me know. Wire me at the Brown Palace in Denver."

After his week-long ordeal of helping Schaffgotsch try to catalogue snow, wind, and whatever else the man was looking for, Hynes wanted to relax. He wanted to go home to his wife, to drop down to his club for a drink, and to chat about the things that really meant something to him—Idaho, Boise, the legislature, and his family.

Back in Boise, Hynes went to the Locker Club, a retreat for local businessmen who wanted to play cards, have a drink, or just escape their families for a few hours. He sat down with a friend, Joe Simmer, director of highways for Idaho.

It was then that Sun Valley was discovered, as William J. Hynes is fond of saying, "over a scotch and soda."

Hynes was eager to tell somebody about the crazy chase the Union Pacific had sent him on. "I told Joe where I'd been and what I'd been through, looking for this ski resort, dragging four or five pairs of skis and ski boots and so on," said Hynes.

When Hynes finished his somewhat incredible story, Simmer looked at him quietly and said, "Did you look in the Hailey and Ketchum area?"

Hynes put his scotch and soda down. The vision of Ketchum and Hailey, clustered near the gateway to the majestic Sawtooth Mountains, came to him.

"By God no," said Hynes. "I forgot."

Hynes sat thinking for a while, nursing his drink, ordering another, and finally saying, "Well, we'd better go down and wire him and tell him to come back here."

Hailey: gateway to Sun Valley country

The telegram was sent, advising Schaffgotsch that there was an area they hadn't tried. If he wished to return, Hynes said, he would show the count the place, a once-prosperous mining area that had fallen on hard times. Hynes knew that, if Schaffgotsch was interested, it would mean another day or two of tramping through Idaho's snow country, but his company loyalty convinced him it was the least he could do for U.P.

Schaffgotsch received the wire with relief. The count had revisited one of the earlier sites and had again come away dissatisfied. Hynes's message was an excuse to put off telling Harriman that there were no appropriate sites in the West, or that if Harriman still wanted to build, it would have to be at a location less than ideal.

Schaffgotsch hurried to the telegraph office and wired Hynes that he would meet him the next day in Shoshone, forty-five miles from Ketchum. For his part, realizing he didn't even know whether the weather would permit entry into Hailey or Ketchum in January, Hynes called the president of the Hailey Chamber of Commerce.

"No," the man said. "We just can't make it. They don't keep the road open from Shoshone to Hailey in January."

Hynes called Joe Simmer. "You got me into this mess," he said; "now you get me out!" The highway director was reassuring. "Go over to Shoshone," Simmer told Hynes, "and I'll get the district engineer, a fellow by the name of Matt Johnson, to take you up there."

Snowbound Ketchum in the thirties

Johnson, Hynes, and Schaffgotsch started for Hailey through ever-deepening snow. By the time they reached Timmerman Hill, they were stuck. Johnson put in a call to Shoshone for a snowplow. The plow arrived, cleared the road, and rammed ahead of the bus containing the intrepid trio and a few other passengers who took advantage of the unscheduled ride. They pushed on, past Bellevue and past Hailey to Ketchum. When the bus stopped, Schaffgotsch stepped out and looked up at the high, heavily wooded mountain standing like a lonely sentinel over the small town. In front of him and to his right, a cluster of smaller, treeless hills flowed back and beyond the town, their slopes smothered in snow. The sky above Schaffgotsch was brilliant blue, and there was no wind.

Hynes and Simmer waited while Schaffgotsch drew in deep breaths of air and walked beside the bus, his boots crunching into the silence. Then, abruptly, Schaffgotsch turned and said he wanted to talk to someone from the area, someone who could lead him to a person who might act as a guide. There was a feeling running through him, a shock wave of possibilities that made him shiver. It was as if someone had lifted a chunk of the lowland Alps from Europe and deposited them at his feet. Maybe, just maybe, he wouldn't have to return to New York City to gaze mournfully at Averell Harriman and tell him the worst. But then, this could be another Jackson Hole or Aspen. He wouldn't know until he had time to go into the land and see what the snow was like.

Hynes took Schaffgotsch to a store run by the Griffith brothers. It was early afternoon by the time they stamped into the frontier emporium, and it was pure luck that they caught the Griffiths at the right time. When winter forced its way into the Sawtooths, Ketchum all but closed down; its meager population of 270 dwindled to about half that number; and the Griffith brothers opened their store just two hours a day.

Hynes approached the man behind the counter. "Do you have a kid around here that can ski pretty good? We've got an Austrian count up here looking for a ski resort."

The grocer looked at Schaffgotsch, dressed in his finest European clothes, and narrowed his eyes. What was a count from Austria doing in Ketchum? In fact, what was a count?

"He's a representative of Mr. Averell Harriman, chairman of the board of the Union Pacific Railroad," Hynes said, and tried to explain the purpose of Schaffgotsch's visit—what exactly a ski resort was and what it would mean to the people of Ketchum.

"Fine," said the grocer, and by sundown everybody in Ketchum knew what Count Felix Schaffgotsch was doing in that remote central Idaho village. They weren't much impressed, but they didn't let their Idaho hospitality crumble completely. Word went down to Jerome, to Jack Lane, owner of the town's general store and one of the most powerful men in the area. Lane was knee-deep in the sheep business, the staple of Ketchum's economy at the time, and he was in the lowlands taking care of his flocks. But he gave a cool appraisal of how the townspeople should treat Schaffgotsch.

"Be nice to him," advised Lane. "But don't cash any of his checks unless the Union Pacific guarantees them."

Schaffgotsch didn't want to cash any checks. All he

wanted was to explore the surrounding hills, study the powder, stand in the crisp air to see if it suddenly turned icy and uncomfortable.

All he wanted from the townspeople was a young man who could lead him through the hills and mountains. The grocer at Griffith Brothers came up with "just the fellow—a good man on skis."

When the young man showed up, Schaffgotsch blinked. "What's that?" he asked.

"My skis," the youngster replied.

Schaffgotsch circled the skis, keeping a straight face. "I've never seen anything like them before," he said. "You ski on these?"

The boy nodded, hugging his skis tightly. They were simple slabs of wood with canvas footholds.

Hynes, tired of waiting for Schaffgotsch and the kid to leave, stepped in. "Just take some of the skis you got here," he said. "You got four or five pair and four or five pair of shoes, and I'm getting damn tired of dragging them around for you."

Schaffgotsch smiled and nodded for the boy to take a pair of skis. Hynes watched as they trudged up Ketchum's main street and stopped to put on the skis; soon they were out of sight.

"They skied around and over those hills for three or four days," said Hynes. The boy would lead Schaffgotsch to the big mountain overlooking Ketchum and to the smaller hills dotting the horizon. They would work their way through the deep powder to a point where Schaffgotsch could look down over the valley,

An Idaho skier

28

where he could see the unbroken vista of snow-covered hills—virgin hills, untouched by alpine skiing. There *was* skiing in the Ketchum area, of course; but it was a basic, cross-country method used simply for getting from house to store, from ranch to school. Alpine skiing, which Schaffgotsch demonstrated for his young guide with a flourish at spots, was something the young boy had never seen.

Hynes and Schaffgotsch had rented a cabin at Bald Mountain Hot Springs. "I waited beside a warm stove for them to come back," said Hynes.

Schaffgotsch would return at night from his treks with little to report of what went on during the day. Finally on the third day, he said, "This looks pretty good," and Hynes breathed a sigh of relief, feeling that home and a warm meal with his wife couldn't be far off.

Ketchum was the place. The powder was dry, the basin at the foot of the towering mountain was practically windless, and the hills immediately surrounding it were a fine size to begin with. And the altitude was good. The area was on the edge of a desert, and yet right at the foot of the craggy Sawtooth Range. That meant mostly sunny days, and if it was going to storm, it would probably storm during the night. The snow? There was plenty of that, Schaffgotsch could see—not too much, but just the right amount.

Schaffgotsch hurried back to Shoshone and wired Harriman in New York City.

"It contains more delightful features," read Schaffgotsch's wire, "than any other place I have seen in the

Cross-country trail

U.S., Switzerland, or Austria for a winter sports center."

Averell Harriman was ready for some good news. But while he felt a tingle of excitement, there was another reaction.

"Skeptical, but interested," Harriman remembers. "I was sure we could find the right place, but I'd been a banker and therefore didn't fall for things too quickly."

Ketchum's "Alps"

Still, Schaffgotsch's attitude was very positive, and he had been straightforward about the other resorts. "He kept us informed of why he felt the different places that he went to were not suitable," said Harriman. "This was the first one that he said he felt was suitable for our purposes. He rang us and went into the records for snowfall and so forth. He found it was very dry snow, not too much snow, and said that it didn't have blizzards. We decided to do something about it. I had this group go out there and we were delighted with it. I began to take it seriously."

Harriman included himself in the group he organized to "go out there." He called for his personal Union Pacific car to be stocked and made ready for the journey.

He also called his good friend William Paley, chairman of the board of the Columbia Broadcasting System. "I took the Paleys along because they were nonskiers. I told him about it and he was interested and amused to go as a vacation." Paley and his wife, Harriman and his younger daughter Mary, and two Austrian skiers headed west within days of Schaffgotsch's wire.

The Paleys loved the area. "They were crazy about it," said Harriman.

So was Harriman.

Before the party arrived, Hynes went out and scavenged about until he found a covered wagon with bent ribs and a canvas over it. He installed a stove in it, and the Paley-Harriman group jumped from the comfort of Harriman's luxurious railroad car to the belly-jangling wagon.

With Schaffgotsch excitedly leading them through the deep snow surrounding Ketchum, the party toured in the covered wagon by day and returned for the night to the cabins at Bald Mountain Hot Springs, where Hynes waited. "I wouldn't have nothing to do with those covered wagons; cold as blazes out there!"

Cold, but beautiful to Averell Harriman. He saw the potential in the little windless valley, the perfect spot to build the ski resort he wanted so badly.

The hills beside the valley, at least the ones on the right-hand side as he looked out from Ketchum, seemed ideal as the foundations for his ski hills. While the hills on the left remained almost bare, the ones on the right glistened with untouched snow. The reason for the dif- ference was that the hills on the left were much lower in elevation than the others and were constantly exposed to the sun.

The search was over. Harriman's faith that some- where in America stood a ski resort just waiting to be built was justified.

"I couldn't believe we wouldn't find it, with all the ski resorts existing in Europe," said Harriman. "I'd learned that a good place to ski required a lot of condi- tions which were not ordinary. I thought we could find a place on the line of the Union Pacific Railroad. I think I assumed that it wasn't going to be very difficult because of the great many ski resorts there were in Switzerland. But our country is so broad and so wide and the conditions are so different. You get these tre- mendous snowfalls, even blizzards, on the west coast. Twenty feet of snow."

While there was plenty of snow at Ketchum, and the Harriman party in fact had to shovel their way to their doors at the Hot Springs, it wasn't the quantity of snow that impressed Schaffgotsch. It was the quality. It was very light and very dry, the kind of powder the count had been dreaming about since he'd left New York.

Nearly thirty years after Averell Harriman had first visited the Ketchum area, working the railroad like any common hired hand, he returned to the same place in his own private car. Harriman was ready to pour mil- lions of dollars into the area and, although it was still too early to predict, make the name Sun Valley famous from Los Angeles to New York City to Tehran.

Union Pacific & Fast Freight Line, 1884

In 1879 the town of Ketchum didn't exist. That year Dave Ketchum, a robust miner used to the deprivations of frontier life, built a cabin along the banks of the Wood River, the stream which wanders through the valley of the same name. There was another man in the area, Albert Gilbert, who stayed there until he died. Ketchum, on the other hand, left after the winter of 1880.

Just the same, the place was named for its first resident—but only after authorities in Washington, D.C., refused to grant the area a post office under its original name, Leadville. The West was crisscrossed with towns named Leadville, small camps that had suddenly become towns with the discovery of gold or silver. Another one, in Idaho, would only confuse things further. So Leadville became Ketchum, even though its namesake had left the hills in search of his fortune in some other area.

Dave Ketchum might have been wiser to stay. The Hailey-Ketchum area, which was then part of a 19,000-square-mile area known as Alturas County, was rich in minerals—one of the richest in the state. Settlers and miners poured into the county, and from 1880 to 1885 over $12 million in lead and silver ore was scooped from the land by scruffy pioneers bent on getting rich quick.

The town flourished. Wells Fargo and Company opened an office in 1881 and soon seven stages were leaving Ketchum for Hailey and other points in the rugged Sawtooth country. By 1883, Ketchum had a telephone system. The following year the Oregon

Before the First Chairlift

. . . Dave Ketchum's Land

Ketchum at the turn of the century

Shortline brought tracks to Ketchum for a daily run, and later became the railroad link that enabled the town to move from a mining economy to one based on sheep ranching. By the time the mines were exhausted, Ketchum had become the northern terminus of the Wood River branch of the Union Pacific; instead of crumbling to dust as a ghost town, Ketchum became the nation's largest sheep-shipping station.

By 1889, the town had reached boom status. There were over 2,000 residents slogging through its muddy streets and tramping through its ramshackle stores and tent bars.

But in 1893, the silver market collapsed, and with it much of Ketchum's startling prosperity. The people turned to sheep ranching, or they turned away from the town altogether. By 1900, the population had dipped to 250, and the citizens had settled down to a peaceful if penny-pinched existence of tranquil summers and snow-bound winters.

But between the boom and the bust, and afterwards, there were exciting times, filled with adventures only the frontier West could spawn.

One of the most colorful accounts of early-day Ketchum was written by Dick d'Easum, a longtime Idaho writer. It appeared in the December 20, 1936, edition of the *Idaho Statesman*, the state's leading newspaper. It was as follows:

"David Ketchum never heard of Sun Valley. He got there 57 years too soon. . . . Much snow has gone under the bridge in the half century between Ketchum's excursion and the creation of a million dollar monument to refrigerated Idaho exercise. . . .

"A Chinese workman and a white prospector have been hanged in the gulch nearby. A grain of wheat in the shoe of Frank Hatton has convicted him of slaying a Hailey merchant. . . . Sawtooth City has ebbed to a population of 600 souls and waned to a hatful of old lumber. Nick the Fiddler and Jimmy de Harp have played generously in Fitzsimmons' Metropolitan saloon for the common customers celebrating the first train journey to Ketchum, while upstairs the leading citizens have waltzed to the tunes of George Delies of the Strauss orchestra, Vienna, Austria.

"David P. Clark, postmaster, has perished in a snowslide near Stanley. Jack Dempsey has been knocked down in a Ketchum saloon. William Finney has charged the Idaho Baptist convention with stealing a church. Andrew W. Mellon has foreclosed a $40,000 mortgage on Hailey property. Broadford miners, working the Minnie Moore and Queen of the Hills, have staged their St. Patrick's day party which required the quieting services of a United States general and a governor.

"Seventeen men have been killed in a snowslide at the North Star mine. The ancestor of all Ketchum cats has been bought from a Chinese by Nellie Easley. Hailey has been burned twice. John D. King has given up his snowshoe mail contract from Bellevue to Bullion. . . .

"Snow has smashed the upper story of the Fitzsim-

Fourth of July, Ketchum, 1924

Fording the stream

mons building while customers rushed from the bar. Postmaster E. B. Williams has stopped a runaway team in the Steward Bros. drug store with the horses' heads in his delivery window. Moses P. Haynes has died with his boots on in the saloon tent. The Alturas hotel, at a cost of $35,000, has been finished and 'admitted to be the finest hotel between Denver and the Pacific ocean.'

"Billy Baxter has shoveled through six feet of snow to dig a grave for Elam Trimm, struck on the head by a tree while skiing from Atlanta to Galena.

"Life has been vigorous at Ketchum. The background of Sun Valley has been hewn from the raw materials of adventure and robust romance. Wood river is old in color, heavy with legend. Yet it is a youngster among Idaho mining camps of similar origin. In 57 years its paragraph of history has been loaded to the guards with red-blooded incidents. . . .

"Beginning of the mining excitement that led to the birth of Ketchum, Bellevue, Hailey, Bullion, Sawtooth, Vienna, Broadford, Muldoon, Zinc, and numerous other mushroom suburbs has been traced to Daniel Scribner's dog that scratched up a fortune in the summer of 1880. As far back as a dozen years before, there had been haphazard prodding into the mineral wealth. It remained for Scribner's dog—the name has been skipped in the records, ungratefully—to rip off the lid.

"The story goes that Scribner was prospecting along Wood river under a grubstake from a man named Moore of Salt Lake. His dog spied a cottontail in a choke-cherry thicket. The rabbit was routed. The dog ran it

Camping near Ketchum

Miners head into the mountains

40

Leadville Mine

41

Fourth of July, 1925

Bald Mountain Hot Springs

into a badger hole and charged down after it, digging furiously in true miner style. Scribner came up to join the fun. He discovered in the tailings behind the disappearing dog, a glint of metal. He staked a claim immediately and named it the Minnie Moore in honor of his grubstaker's daughter. He sold his interest to Moore, Miller and Myers. The mine produced between 10 and 15 million dollars, principally in silver. Gold has

never been an important metal on Wood river. . . .

"Mortgage trouble lowered the boom in 1887. The Philadelphia and Idaho company picked up the pieces along with a string of mines, including two on Boyle mountain, and another smelter at Muldoon. The second venture cracked in 1893 when the price of silver fell out of sight. Aside from several million dollars in payrolls, Ketchum got from the proposition the honor

Sun Valley Lead-Silver Mines, Inc.

of having the first electric light plant in the territory. The smelter was lighted by electricity. Hailey had the first town system and the first telephone system. . . .

"The Sawtooth country has always prided itself on big game. Biggest game hunt was in 1883. The bag was an elephant.

"'Samson,' cantankerous brute shown by Cole brothers' circus at Hailey, took a walk. Although hobbled fore and aft, he upset a lion cage as a starter, ripped through his tent, pushed over an ore car, and utterly ignored his trainer close behind and yelling every step for Samson to lie down. Donald McKay stepped to the rescue.

"'I pulled my .44,' he said, 'and stepped up to the trainer.

"'Will it hurt him, I says. No, says the trainer. So I let Samson have it. Pumped 12 shots into his hide. Never stopped walking. Didn't even let on he was shot.'

"The elephant, somewhat piqued, no doubt, by such treatment, hauled up a section of Quigley ranch fence and tossed it at the posse, which by that time included several men with revolvers, all banging away full blast. Farmers prodded Samson with pitchforks. He just went on walking and hauling up fence. Finally the trainer obtained a crowbar, heated one end and thrust it into Samson's mouth. He squealed, gave up the battle, and returned calmly to his quarters. He lived several years, finally to be executed for violence in the east.

"A spot near Quigley's ranch was also the scene of a different sort of sport. It was in Hangman's gulch, first gulch north, that George Pierson and Kuok Wah Choi—Ah Sam—were hanged. Pierson was executed August 1, 1884 . . . for the murder of John T. Hall, generally known as Johnny-Behind-the-Rocks, a Vienna prospector believed to have found a rich pocket. The story goes that he so infuriated men who followed him by popping out from behind boulders and thumbing his

Comic baseball team, Ketchum, 1917

nose, that he was slain. The killing occurred October 24, 1882. Pierson's trial was prolonged over two years.

"Another notable shooting, on the reliable word of the *Hailey Times,* was the fracas in which Charley Moore, proprietor of the Alturas hotel, emptied his weapon at Colonel Russell of the *Wood River Times,* wounded the editor in the neck and shoulder, and drilled his new hotel all six times.

"The shooting in 1886, as the *Times* records it, resulted from a bit in Russell's paper to the effect that Hotelman Moore didn't pay his bills. Moore met the gentleman of the press just outside the Alturas bar room, held one hand on his shoulder, and fired with the other. Editor Russell, the paper says, was somewhat

Ketchum panorama

under the effect of refreshment dispensed at the bar, and lurched evasively, spoiling Moore's aim. The editor's wounds were slight but the damage to the hotel was considerable. . . .

"When the matter came to trial the magistrate fined Moore $100 for assault and admonished, 'If I hear any more instances of such bad shooting they shall be dealt with severely.' . . .

"Whether Jack Dempsey was actually knocked off his pins at Ketchum is a disputed question. There are many, however, who will bear out the report that he trained there in his early fighting days. The Manassa mauler divided his time between the mines and the ring. The scene of his alleged knockdown was the Fitzsimmons saloon, where everything happened. The name of the place apparently inspired him. . . ."

Ketchum's Main Street

By 1936, however, the town's violent and exciting days were far behind it. The tent saloons had been folded before the turn of the century, and while an occasional cowboy might get a little too excited on a Saturday night, the frontier aura of violence and gunplay had diminished.

It was to this little corner of snow and woods that Roberta Brass returned in January of 1936. She had

Jack Dempsey

been in Los Angeles for several months, a young working girl who had forsaken the hills of Idaho for the flatlands of Hollywood. She missed the hills, and her father's ranch which lay nestled among them a mile or two outside Ketchum.

Roberta Brass Garretson doesn't remember the exact day she arrived; she just knows it was in a bus escorted by a snowplow, and that she was in the company of a rather distinguished-looking gentleman whom others on the bus constantly referred to as "the count." At the time, she gave it little thought.

Several days later, Roberta heard the news sweeping through Ketchum that a young Austrian count was seeking a place to build a ski resort for the president of the mighty Union Pacific Railroad. Roberta remembered the young man on the bus, and so it didn't surprise her terribly when one day, as she was sitting on her father's corral fence, he should suddenly appear on cross-country skis.

"He recognized me," said Mrs. Garretson. "He mentioned that he had been in Canada and Colorado and that he was now looking over the Idaho territory of the Union Pacific; that he was a scout for Averell Harriman."

That particular day, Schaffgotsch was out on his skis testing weather conditions and area temperatures. He told Roberta he was extremely pleased with the area.

A day or two later the two met again. Schaffgotsch told Roberta that it looked like the Ketchum country might be the place for the resort. At the moment, he

Early skiers, Wood River Valley

48

said, he was searching for the ideal location for the lodge. He wanted the area in the valley where the warmest air currents flowed. That would be the place where the lodge would be located.

"I laughed and I said, you know when the weather gets cold, I always notice the stock going to this particular spot," said Mrs. Garretson.

Schaffgotsch asked where that spot might be, since naturally, if the cows were huddling there on cold days, it must have meant that was the warmest place in the valley. Roberta pointed out the area and Schaffgotsch bowed, saying, "That is the area I selected."

With Harriman's departure, Schaffgotsch stayed on in Ketchum for several days and then left, only to return later with another Austrian, whom Mrs. Garretson remembers only as Count Wilheilm. Schaffgotsch was sure the Ketchum area was the right spot, but he wanted a second opinion.

Schaffgotsch and Wilheilm skied across the country, sometimes escorted by Roberta Brass and her sister Marjorie. Once, the two sisters took the two Austrians on an early morning coyote hunting expedition. When the Austrians arrived, carrying their fancy European-made cross-country skis, they were wide-eyed when the two sisters brought out their own Idaho-made skis. They were even stranger than the pair Schaffgotsch had seen belonging to the young boy at the Griffith Brothers grocery.

"Marjorie and I were using the old-type Ketchum skis the old miners used," said Roberta. "They were

A single pole helped early skiers steer and stop

about eleven-foot skis with a canvas housing packed around them and a heavy leather guard to keep your feet from sliding around.''

To push themselves along, the Brass sisters each carried a broken pitchfork handle. "The Austrians just howled; they had never seen anything like it before in their lives,'' said Roberta. "The only brake you had going downhill was the pitchfork handle.''

Wilheilm agreed that the Ketchum area would be ideal for a ski resort. Soon Harriman's engineers moved in, and Roberta Brass was one of those asked to guide them around the canyons, washes, and flatlands surrounding the remote Idaho town.

Time was passing.

Back in New York City, Averell Harriman approached the Board of Directors of the Union Pacific Railroad and told them his plan and that he was on the verge of implementing it. There were no loud groans or cries of folly.

"I was the chairman of the board and the board went along," said Harriman. "It was a relatively small investment for the railroad. It was a great big railroad with a great big income."

To build the resort, Harriman needed land, and the land Schaffgotsch selected belonged to Roberta's father. Ernest Brass owned 3,500 acres of grazing land near Ketchum and the grazing rights to a large tract, from the top of Trail Creek Summit to the Hyndman Peaks.

Ernest Brass sat in his ranch house while the mighty law department of Union Pacific marched through his front door. Judge Joseph J. McFadden, a native of Hailey and Chief Justice of the Idaho Supreme Court, remembers the negotiations because his father, who was also a lawyer, helped the Brass attorney.

"You have to understand the way the Union Pacific worked," McFadden said. "They had a land department in the Union Pacific, they had a tax department and they had an engineering department. They were the ones who handled the negotiations."

The depression wasn't a time for a man to ponder over an offer—especially an offer for his land—and Ernest Brass barely had time to see if the snow was melting before the whirl of Union Pacific representatives had him signing away his ranch.

"Those were pretty depressed years," his daughter recalls. "Any rancher or sheepman was really struggling. Considering it meant selling in a whole block and not parceling anything out, it sounded logical. And then, the property wasn't much, because you have short growing seasons there. In fact, it was necessary at the ranch, the few years they tried to calve or lamb out, to go down to the lower land, to the Hagerman Valley. It was just too cold. I can remember having to carry cottonseed cake out to keep them alive."

But Harriman didn't care about the growing season. In fact, the shorter the growing season the better. Short growing seasons meant long winters.

In the end, Ernest Brass signed over his land for a little over one dollar an acre. He was not a tough negotiator, and besides, he was looking forward to retirement in Jerome, a town about 100 miles from Ketchum in the fertile Magic Valley. Brass was unaware that the time would come when land less suited for development than his would be going for prices that would have made him a wealthy man in the 1930's. The land he sold for a little more than $4,300 would be worth millions of dollars forty years later.

But in 1936, not even Averell Harriman nor Count Felix Schaffgotsch really envisioned what Sun Valley would become to the world—and how much the world would come to Sun Valley.

Sun Valley . . . in the Idaho wilderness

During February and March the snow remained on Ketchum's hills and mountains, refusing to surrender to the sagebrush and brown dirt which lay under its smooth cover. The townspeople waited for the influx of Union Pacific officials to direct the building of the new resort they had been promised. They waited, not entirely convinced that vast amounts of railroad money would really begin flowing into their crippled economy and once again fire the town to a life in the tradition of the boom-time 1880's.

But the U.P. did come. As the snow melted, the little Shoshone-Ketchum branch of the Union Pacific began feeding tools, machinery and people into the area, and construction began on Sun Valley.

Harriman, conscious that he could build a ski resort in the middle of an Idaho wilderness and nobody outside Ketchum would know about it, had hired as his public relations director Steve Hannagan, one of the country's top promotion men. Hannagan visited the Ketchum area before the first earth was turned to build the lodge. He hated it. He was by nature a warm-weather creature. Legend has it that Hannagan was about to turn his back on the whole project when the temperature rose to ninety degrees without melting the snow. The story is fable, of course, since if the thermometer hovers at about fifty or sixty degrees for too many days in a row at Sun Valley, the snow melts, just like snow anywhere else. But it did get quite warm; and the sun, the blue skies, and the abundance of snow swayed Hannagan. The promoter in him started work-

Of Bananas and Other Things

. . . Construction Begins

Photo for original Sun Valley poster

ing. He foresaw a campaign centered around a young man stripped to the waist, standing in powder snow, a blazing sun beating down on his tanned back and his smile enticing the viewer to come to this sunny place among the slopes. Indeed, that was the thrust of Hannagan's publicity campaign, and the poster of just such a young man gave the resort instant identification.

Harriman hired Gilbert, Stanley, Underwood and Company of Los Angeles as architects and ground was broken in May, 1936, for the Sun Valley Lodge—but not the lodge that Harriman had originally projected. With Hannagan at his side, throwing ideas at him for a resort containing all the elements of roughing it in supreme luxury, Harriman had become convinced that a rustic little lodge in the middle of nowhere wouldn't be all that "new."

"Our first thought was to have a small lodge, to try it out and see how it would work," said Harriman. "I think Steve was among those who suggested that if you're going to get publicity you've got to have a million-dollar hotel in the middle of the mountains. *That* would be news. So we built the lodge first, and there was tremendous publicity about it."

By June, construction was underway at full tilt. When news of the job opportunities available in the Ketchum area spread through the mountains and valleys of south-central Idaho, men began arriving on horses, in trucks and cars, and on foot to sign on with the Union Pacific's work crews.

Pete Lane, the young high-school-aged son of Jack

Lane (the man who first insisted no one cash Count Schaffgotsch's checks), was there. "The rumor got out that the contractors were going to start building, and the streets and everything else were just jammed with cars," Pete said. "People wanted to sign up to try and get an appointment up here."

The foreman for the operation and most of the skilled people were brought in from the Los Angeles area. But a great many of the laborers were from the Ketchum area, pumping up its economy greatly.

Everything was going smoothly. The resort lacked just two things—a way to get skiers up the mountains, and a name.

The latter was easily taken care of, although there's a minor dispute over who came up with the name. Harriman is said by many, including himself, to have named it, while early Sun Valley press releases give the honor to Hannagan. A third candidate might be Felix Schaffgotsch, who all along said he was searching for a place where the sun continually shone.

Actually, there was some experimentation before "Sun Valley" was decided upon. Roberta Garretson remembers that names like "Back Pay" (an old mining claim), "Glass Ford," "Hyndman Peaks," and "Trail Creek" were tossed around, but none of them very seriously. "Sun Valley" seemed logical and, regardless of who gets the credit for it, the name ultimately belongs to all the men who sweated through that summer of 1936, carving a small bit of Europe into the silent Idaho mountains.

A cold but game Steve Hannagan rides a lift

Work in progress

56

That left the problem of finding a new method of transporting skiers up the steep slopes—a method that would be unique enough to give Sun Valley a pioneering image from the start.

It was Steve Hannagan's suggestion that the U.P.'s engineering department tackle the problem. Hannagan's memo to Averell Harriman spoke of "mechanical devices . . . to take people to the top of the slides." The engineers looked at several "mechanical devices," including a j-bar that had been installed at Bromley, Vermont, and an up-ski toboggan in use at Yosemite, California. Both of these had their drawbacks; for one, neither could transport a large number of people to the top. A cable car was also considered before a young engineer stepped in with an idea so unique, so startling, that it was almost rejected.

The young man's contribution to the skiing industry revolutionized the sport, yet his name is all but unknown.

Jim Curran invented the chairlift.

Before joining Union Pacific, where he would later rise to the rank of chief engineer, Curran had worked for the Paxton and Vierling Iron Works in Omaha. One of the firm's contracts had been to install devices to load bananas on fruit boats in South America. The method of the day was a davit-and-hook affair that lifted the bunches in single loads from the dock to the hold. Curran envisioned a kind of conveyor system that would give the boat a continuous flow of cargo, and a variation on this is what he now had in mind to keep Sun Valley

W. A. Harriman, Steve Hannagan

Nearing completion

skiers moving up the mountains to the top.

His superiors said it was too hazardous.

The idea might have died there, lost forever, had not Charley Proctor rescued it. Proctor, one of America's foremost pioneer skiers and a former ski star at Dartmouth, had been hired to help lay out the runs at Sun Valley. On his way west, Proctor stopped at the railroad's headquarters to see what progress had been made in regard to the matter of getting the skiers up the hills. When Proctor showed up at the office, the message went out for Curran to bring "everything you have" for Proctor to peruse.

Curran took the order quite literally. The idea of the banana-lift had died hard with him—in fact hadn't died at all—so despite the earlier rejection by his immediate superiors, Curran slipped the sketch into the stack of papers. Maybe Charley Proctor would see the design as something more than simply hazardous.

Proctor did. He found the idea of a lift utilizing a chair intriguing, and told the engineering staff that was his choice.

Word soon reached Averell Harriman that his engineers had developed something extraordinary—and workable, at least in the eyes of Charley Proctor and Jim Curran. After going over the plans with several ski experts, whose numbers included his close friend, financier J.P. Morgan, Harriman made his decision. The monocable, as it was called, would be developed further and tested.

Whipped into Curran's corner by Harriman's order,

Charles Proctor

Test chair, Omaha

the engineers soon had a working model ready at the Union Pacific's Omaha headquarters. Morgan himself, who was to spend a great deal of time at Sun Valley in its early years, went to Omaha to test the new chair. The trial involved an old pickup truck which had been fitted with a chair hanging from its side. Morgan was told to stand on a bed of straw—wearing his skis—and be ready for the chair to pick him up. It didn't work, and so somebody suggested Morgan put on roller skates for better movement. It worked. The experiments started with the pickup pulling the chair at a rate of four feet a minute. Soon it was increased to fifty and eventually to 450 feet a minute—safely!

Jim Curran (who also designed the footrests used on the Sun Valley lifts) never skied. He wanted to try it, but an untimely accident kept him off skis. While racing another engineer on Sun Valley's new ice rink, Curran fell and broke his arm. The accident provoked an immediate directive from the Union Pacific head office that no employee of the railroad could take part in any winter sports—skiing or ice-skating—unless it was absolutely necessary to his job. The rule was later rescinded, but not until Curran's passion for learning to ski had subsided. Just the same, the nonskier is memorialized on the valley's towering Bald Mountain; in the early 1960's, a section of the mountain was named "Curran's Corner," in honor of the imaginative young man whose tenacity changed the world of skiing.

While work on the lodge progressed, Harriman and his people began selecting the hills to be used for ski-

Man and chairlift meet—successfully

Dollar Mountain lift

ing. After careful consideration, three hills within walk-ing distance of the lodge were selected. They were to be named Ruud, Proctor (for Charley Proctor), and Dollar mountains; and lifts of the single chair variety were to be built up their sides. In 1936, if a skier could master Dollar Mountain, a veritable anthill compared to the European monsters, he was considered an expert.

Bald Mountain, solemn and forever brooding over the valley, was bypassed. At first the general opinion was that Schaffgotsch and Harriman didn't consider it suit-able for development, but that wasn't the case. Schaffgotsch had traveled the mountain and marveled at the variety it could offer. But he was wise in knowing that in the beginning, the number of skiers good enough to handle Baldy would be too small to make its immediate development feasible. Once Sun Valley got going, became a success, and started drawing and turn-ing out skiers capable of negotiating steeper trails, Bald Mountain would be a skiers' paradise.

Ketchum was changing. Not since the days of the mining boom, when soiled miners slapped down hard-earned money for a drink, had Ketchum seemed so alive. Pete Lane, a wide-eyed seventeen-year-old at the time, found the change spellbinding.

"You couldn't believe it. The bars started opening up, and of course they had wide-open gambling in those days," said Lane. "It was the hot spot in the state, let's put it that way. There wasn't too much construc-tion going on then in our state. I remember our old store. It turned from just a sheepherders' place into—

Madeleine Carroll ski run, Proctor Mountain

well, with all the construction people around, you just couldn't believe it."

Labor was cheap for Union Pacific. Men wanted jobs and so they were willing to work for forty-three cents an hour and full bellies at night. Union Pacific fed them well, and many of the crews who came to help build the resort stayed on from the day it opened until many years later.

The lodge was taking shape. The impressive facility rose steadily, its rustic exterior formed not by trees from the forested countryside, but by cement poured into pinewood forms. This was done for several reasons—first of all, longevity. A lodge constructed of wood couldn't possibly have lasted thirty or forty years under the heavy wear and tear of the tourists and the elements. Second, there was potential fire hazard. When Sun Valley was constructed, Ketchum had a meager fire department, one that would have been ineffectual against a blaze any bigger than one in the fireplace of the lodge dining room.

So the lodge was cast in cement, but as it turned out—and those in charge of construction didn't plan it this way—what emerged from the forms was so unique that few people could tell it from the real thing. The cement had hardened and expanded against the pine forms, and when they were knocked away, the lodge had taken on a color and texture that gave it the appearance of having been constructed from real trees.

While the McNeil Construction Company of Los Angeles was pushing construction of the lodge, and young Pete Lane was busy courting McNeil's daughter Jeanne (whom he later married), William Castagnetto, one of U.P.'s crack bridge engineers, was waiting to take charge of the lift construction. By August the lifts had been readied, and so on August 26 Castagnetto and his crew began the tedious work of snaking the devices up Dollar and Proctor mountains. By November, the first chairlifts up Dollar and Proctor were completed.

For a few breathless minutes during the first test on Proctor, there was some question about the lifts. Two women, one of them Florence Law, secretary to the manager of Sun Valley, had volunteered to ride the chair on its inaugural trip. But a fuse blew, leaving the ladies stranded high above the anxious onlookers. Eventually the fuse was replaced, and Law, acting under boss's orders, stayed on alone and rode the chair to the top. A new era in skiing had begun.

Soon, however, those lifts on Proctor and Dollar mountains were to seem about as daring and controversial as an early one-reel motion picture. Just as the big-screen adventures would replace the Keystone Cops, so would Dollar and Proctor be one-upped by their large friend, Bald Mountain.

"That was Schaffgotsch's ambition, to go up there and build the finest lifts anywhere," recalled Harriman. "And that is one of the finest ski mountains anywhere. It has open slopes and it has runs in all directions, and you can usually find skiing someplace where it's safe. My experience at Sun Valley, when I was first there, was that—let's say the skiing wasn't very good. Well,

Chairlift from Dollar Cabin

The finished lodge

Going up (Dollar lift)

Coming down—Charley Proctor

Bald Mountain before the first lift

I'd get one of the guides to take me out and find some-place where the skiing *was* good."

One summer day in 1938, when he still hadn't really committed himself to building a lift on Baldy, Harriman was out on horseback with Castagnetto. "He wanted me to take him up Warm Springs [part of Baldy], close to the summit there," Castagnetto recalled. "He was still looking for ski territory. As we came back, he had me stop on the north side of Bald Mountain. He stopped there, and he said, 'I have skied all over Europe and there isn't a mountain that will do what Bald Mountain will do.' See, he visualized the whole thing."

Castagnetto's main job in the late thirties was bridge and building superintendent for Union Pacific. As a result, his work took him away from Sun Valley most of the time. But whenever Harriman wanted something done to improve the resort, he called Castagnetto back. He was called from Washington state in May of 1937, for example, to create a lake near the lodge for boating and fishing. Harriman wanted it finished by July 1, the summer opening date. Castagnetto built the required dam and gave Harriman his lake, on schedule.

In 1939, a year after that talk on the mountain, Harriman wired Castagnetto to proceed to Sun Valley. When he arrived, he found that Harriman wanted to take another ride up Baldy, this time with two other companions: a man named Bannerman, from American Steel and Wire, and a man named Trout, a Union Pacific bridge engineer. Castagnetto had a feeling Harriman hadn't called him to Sun Valley because

The view from Baldy—Toni Frissell

there was an extra horse.

"Mr. Harriman said he wanted to go up on Bald Mountain, so we each got a saddle horse and went. And so we set on a little knoll where the Roundhouse [restaurant] is now. Mind you, this is all timber down there; you can't see where you are going or anything else. You have no profile, you have no survey, you have no plans drawn, you have no motors, no towers, no rollers. Mr. Harriman sat there a long time and said, 'I'd like to build a chairlift here, down through there and up to the top of the mountain.' So we set there and talked a little while. Mind you, we didn't have a survey. And he said to Mr. Trout, 'I'd like to have an estimate by six o'clock tonight.'"

Trout took the news in silence, never for a minute thinking he should question Harriman's judgment. But Castagnetto knew what was racing through his mind. It would be tough.

"Well, gee whiz, you don't know what your towers are going to look like, you don't know anything," said Castagnetto, "how much concrete goes in for the footings or anything."

But the three of them huddled—Trout, Castagnetto, and Bannerman. Trout instructed Castagnetto to figure out the amount of concrete needed and the cost of the labor; Bannerman, the cost of the steel; and Trout would work out the cost of motors and tramline.

By six that night, the trio approached Harriman and told him their estimate was for $205,000. The money was appropriated, the crew brought in, and soon they

Averell Harriman in fresh powder

The Roundhouse

Lunch in the Roundhouse

Ski instruction, Dollar Mountain

were waging war with the mountain to get the three-stage lift built by winter.

Lloyd Castagnetto, William's son, was a member of the crew that helped construct the lifts on Baldy. "In order to complete it, they started from the top, just opposite of what every other construction job would do," he said. "They had to do that so as to beat the snows and have the top done when the snow hit there. As a result, it was a fantastic job in developing logistics and building trams and getting the men and equipment and the materials up."

"I hit it three ways," explained his father. "I had a crew at the bottom working up, and I put two other crews right below where the Roundhouse is now. Every old timer up there that had been there all their life said you'll never get it finished. The snow will run you off of there before you are finished and you'll never do it. Looking back on it, some of the jobs looked almost impossible to get done, but we did it—by Thanksgiving! We had only a little snow, and by Thanksgiving I had most of the chairs up."

Although they budgeted the lift at $205,000, they brought it in for about $185,000, a relatively small sum considering Union Pacific would pour over three million dollars into Sun Valley the first three years—and considering the fact that, forty years later, that same lift would have cost more than $800,000.

William Castagnetto was pleased the project had been completed at below the budgeted amount, but he wasn't about to let that extra $20,000 fall back into the railroad treasury. Not when he could put it to good use.

So when Charley Davidson, a Boise man in charge of landscaping the resort for Union Pacific, and Pat Rogers, the manager of the area in 1939, approached him with the idea of building some kind of shelter, a restaurant, or perhaps a bar, on the mountain, Castagnetto was ready to help.

"Charley said, 'I'll get the rafters,' and Pat says 'I've got a stone mason working down at the Grand Canyon and I'll bring him up here and we'll put a four-way fireplace in the center,'" said Castagnetto.

When they had finished, the three had created the Roundhouse, an octagon-shaped restaurant high on Baldy, with forty-six windows from which to stare at the valley below and the neighboring Sawtooths, which seemed close enough to cut. The rafters and the material for the gigantic fireplace were no problem for Castagnetto, but the windows drew some protests.

"I had to order those windows from Omaha, and when I sent in the word, I immediately got a wire back that said, 'What the hell are you going to do with forty-six windows?!' But they sent them and we got it done. Mr. Harriman came out then," Castagnetto continued, "and he rode up and he liked it so well that he's the one who named it the Roundhouse."

Before Baldy and well before the Roundhouse, Sun Valley opened. It opened December 21, 1936—and if a grand opening of any sort in that era was unusual, the grand opening of a ski resort was unheard of. For the people of Idaho especially, it was a time to stop and take

Lodge staff, opening season

Back of the lodge

stock of what was happening.

One of its more literate natives did just that. Inez Callaway Robb, who grew up in Boise and became a top syndicated columnist in the forties and fifties, was writing for the *New York Herald Tribune's* women's department then. Robb sat down at her typewriter and clattered out a story that told of the impending festivities.

"It's only a matter of hours until the slopes of the Sawtooth mountains, as respectable a range as there is in the Rockies, will be covered with prominent citizens from New York, Hollywood, and intermediate points. Movie actresses, Wall Street financiers, debutantes, Men-About-Town and society matrons, all with hickory bed slats strapped to their feet, will be falling up hill and down dale on their expensive faces. And all pour la sport. The sport is skiing and the place, so help me, is my own, my lovely Idaho.

"Society with a capital 'S' is on a par with termites. It gets into everything. Nothing is sacred, not even the Sawtooths. One day a place is Ketchum, dedicated to free air and the supposition that any man is apt to stop off on his way to Galena. And the next thing you know, the spot has been rechristened Sun Valley and transformed into a resort to trap the dude population. There seems little doubt now that what was once Ketchum is about to become a Center of Fashion on a plane with Palm Beach, Southampton, Aiken, St. Moritz and Palm Springs.

"This is indeed a mixed blessing. Prominent people who are always getting their pictures in the rotogravure section are a funny lot. They know surprising little about the facts of life outside a 27-room apartment with 15 baths and two butlers. The good people of Ketchum had best make up their minds right now to being regarded as 'quaint' and 'natives.' And they'd better prepare themselves to answer the damnedest assortment of questions that ever have come their way. Also, to contain—as best they can—their laughter the first time they spot a skier in his full and fashionable habiliments.

"There is only one error into which I, as a true daughter of the west, entreat the citizens of Ketchum and its environs not to fall. Don't make the mistake of regarding the dude visitors as effete easterners or Prettified Percys. Any way you look at it, skiing is man's work, even when it's done by women. There may be a trace of insanity, but there's no touch of the sissy in any individual who deliberately slides down mountains on two narrow planks—with the possibility of wrapping himself around several evergreens en route. Thanks, but I'd rather break broncs. Who wants to spend the winter picking pine needles out of his system?

"But there's no doubt that thousands of personages are willing to do just that. This nation within the last three years has become ski crazy. Apparently the whole country has been waiting not for the end of unemployment and the flush of prosperity, but for the dawn of a new day in which such a magnificent ski paradise as Sun Valley would burgeon on the horizon.

"'I don't know where we're going to put them all,'

Mr. and Mrs. Sam Goldwyn

says Mr. William Averell Harriman happily as he fingers the piles of applications for room and board at the de luxe new hotel near Ketchum. Youthful, good-looking Mr. Harriman has a double stake in the hotel as president of the Union Pacific railroad and as chairman of the board of governors of the Sun Valley Ski club. One can almost hear him mentally enlarging the hotel to twice or thrice its present size, in response to popular demand. (I wonder if he could detect my mental hope that the customers, after paying the Union Pacific for transportation and board and lodging, will have enough left over to do a little vicarious spending in and for Idaho?)

"It will be impossible for Mr. Harriman and his pretty wife, the former Marie Norton Whitney, to be on hand for the formal opening of the hotel on December 21. They'll probably go to Sun Valley early in the new year. Social duties keep them in New York in the meantime. Mr. Harriman's younger daughter, Mary, is making her debut this season. Since the Christmas holidays are the gayest days of the deb season, the Harrimans will remain in New York to see that Mary has her share of the fun. Then, with Mary, they'll pack their mitts and muffs and be off for Sun Valley.

"Marie Harriman as well as her husband will leave a job behind when she heads for Idaho. This extremely attractive and petite brunette, who was the first wife of Cornelius Vanderbilt (Sonny) Whitney, conducts a fashionable art gallery of her own in East Fifty-seventh street. She was in Idaho late last summer with Mr. Har-

riman when the hotel was under construction. It's interesting to know that she went with reluctance, and then literally had to be drug back to Manhattan from a spot with which she fell in love and which she thinks is one of the most beautiful in the world.

"Both the Harrimans are so crazy about Sun Valley and have talked about it so much that all their Park avenue acquaintances are in a fine frenzy to see the resort. Tommy Hitchcock, jr., probably the best known of all American polo players, is taking his winter vacation in Sun Valley. His tall, slim, dark wife (one of the Mellons of the Pittsburgh Mellons) is going along.

"Undoubtedly the biggest social catches already bagged for Sun Valley are Mrs. Vincent Astor and her sister-in-law, Mrs. Raimund von Hofmannstahl, the former Alice Muriel Astor. They're going out sometime during the season. So is Mr. von Hofmannstahl, an Austrian by birth and hence a polished performer on skiis [sic]. All Austrians are born skiiers, which is the reason the Sun Valley Ski school is manned by handsome gents of this nationality. I have never seen the blonde, graceful Mrs. Astor on skiis and it's my hunch she's going out to Sun Valley to look rather than to leap. But the Von Hofmannstahls doubtless will be all over the slopes.

"Bobby Lehman, a cousin of Governor Herbert Lehman of New York, will try the Sawtooths, and so will the Douglas Burdens. (It was the Clan Burden which loaned a Long Island residence to H.R.H., the Prince of Wales, who lately has decided love is more important than a crown, when he visited this country in 1924.)

"Roland Palmedo, president of the Amateur Ski club of New York, and Mrs. Palmedo wouldn't miss the new ski center for a perfect geländesprung. Mr. and Mrs. Artemus L. Gates and Mr. and Mrs. Ward Cheney have signed up, too. Mrs. Gates and Mrs. Cheney are daughters of the late Henry P. Davison, a partner of J.P. Morgan & Co. and national president of the American Red Cross during the World war.

"Times change so rapidly that before long it may be impossible for a cat to look at a king. But if he can possibly get away from his task of running Rockefeller Centre, it will be possible for skiiers to look at Nelson A. Rockefeller this winter. The second son of John D. Rockefeller, jr., is a graduate of Dartmouth college, which is the same as saying that he knows his way about on skiis. Dartmouth has produced more excellent skiiers than any other institution in the east. Young Mr. Rockefeller is a governor of the Sun Valley Ski club. So is another Dartmouth graduate, Charles N. Proctor of Boston, who has trained the staff of Idaho guides who'll ride herd on adventurous visitors in Sun Valley.

"Other governors of the Sun Valley Ski club include Alexander H. Bright of Boston, John W. Hanes of New York, and Robert E. Pabst of Milwaukee's famous beer family. All are expected at Sun Valley during the season.

"Sometime during the winter—she doesn't know just when—Mrs. Eddy Duchin, the former Marjorie Oel-

Julius Fleischmann

81

Starlet Laurie Lane "ice tanning"

82

richs of the Newport Oelrichses, will return to Sun Valley. She wants to see how the customers are taking to the new hotel for whose interior decoration she is responsible from cellar to garret. Before she married the widely-known orchestra leader, Marjorie-of-the-Greta-Garbo bob had earned a comfortable living as an interior decorator.

"After her marriage, Mrs. Duchin gave up her career. Then the Harrimans asked for her advice on the decoration of Sun Valley lodge, and, before she realized it, she was doing the whole job. It's doubtful if dark, gloomy-looking Mr. Duchin (the perfect phizz for Hamlet) will be able to make the trip west. He has too many engagements in the east, but the orchestra which will play sweet and hot for guests at the lodge was hand-picked for the job by Mr. Duchin.

"Dolly Schiff Baker, A. Charles Schwartz, whose racing stable is so swell; Fred Osborn, Fred M. Warburg, of the artistically and financially talented Warburgs; John E. Parson and Prince Serge Obolensky, Russia's so handsome gift to America, are other New Yorkers contemplating the trek west to Idaho.

"All Hollywood, it appears, is champing at the bit, impatient to descend on Sun Valley by the train load.

"'Hollywood is moving up to Sun Valley for New Year's eve. We expect at least a train load of 'em,' Mr. Harriman's office said a few days ago.

"Merian Cooper has engaged rooms for a party of 10 and Dave Selznick for a party of eight. Sam Goldwyn, Hollywood's most famous dialectician, will probably be among the New Year's revelers.

"Long, rangy Gary Cooper, whose screen romances keep feminine pulses at 10 above par, is taking his winter vacation at Sun Valley. His extremely attractive young wife, the former Veronica Balfe of New York, will be with him. Mrs. Cooper, who is a niece of Dolores del Rio, had a brief screen career as Sandra Shaw. Claudette Colbert, among Hollywood's No. 1 glamour girls, has signed up for Sun Valley, too.

"Margot Taft is going out from Cincinnati; William A.P. Pullman and J. Sanford Otis from Chicago; Julius Fleischmann, of the yeast and gin Fleischmanns, from Cincinnati; Louis Hill from St. Paul; Richard P. Gale and his family from Minneapolis and Mrs. Bill Paley, wife of the president of the Columbia Broadcasting system, from Manhattan. She's young and most attractive. So is Mr. Paley. If she likes Sun Valley, it's dollars to doughnuts she'll lure her husband out to Idaho, too. And how could anyone fail to like the towering Sawtooths?

"The persons who're going to Sun Valley from Manhattan are those who set the styles and determine what is and isn't fashionable in clothes, liquor, travel, recreation and resorts. Once they've placed the stamp of their glittering approval on Idaho's de luxe ski paradise, I foresee the state as well as the Sawtooths overrun with so-called city slickers.

"Frankly, Sun Valley is doing more to advertise Idaho throughout the nation than all her local chambers of commerce could hope to do in the next 20 years.

Salute to the sun—spring on the mountain

Ski forest on Baldy

As an exile from home, I have often felt that Idaho is not so much the Forgotten as the Unknown state. The times I've lost my temper trying to explain where and what it is! Heretofore Idaho has been chiefly famous for three products in the order of their importance: Baked Potatoes, Earl Sande and Senator Borah. I have a hunch that Sun Valley is going to put us on the map at last.

"Society is like a band of sheep. Get a few bell-wethers, such as I've named above, headed in a certain direction and the rest will surely clamber after. Doubtless Idaho will soon be included on Society's annual circuit, and the woods will be full of Vanderbilts, Astors, Belmonts, Goulds and what-nots.

"In addition to its countless beauties, Sun Valley has one invaluable attraction over all other fashionable resorts north or south. One can obtain a sun tan twice as quickly sliding up and down the Sawtooths as lying on the sands of Palm Beach. This may seem a frivolous reason. But anyone who tries to keep up with the Park avenue Joneses knows that a nut brown tan, comparable to an old saddle bag, is the most envied sign of aristocracy in the east during the off, or out-of-sun, months."

Opening festivities—Claudette Colbert

By the middle of December, 1936, Sun Valley was being referred to by some of the outsiders who had come in to whip it into shape as the "Ketchum Con."

Steve Hannagan, the whiz-kid promotion man, had done his job well. The word was out to the world about Sun Valley, and high-quality, big-name guests were assured. The resort had an outdoor ice rink, heated swimming pool, million-dollar lodge, and the might of Union Pacific behind it to make its emergence as a ski resort a very newsy event throughout the country.

But in the second week of December, 1936, the name "Ketchum Con" seemed appropriate. Indeed, it seemed that Felix Schaffgotsch must have used mirrors or props when he sold the place to Averell Harriman back in January of that year.

There was no snow.

When the wind blew over Dollar and Proctor mountains, it rattled through clumps of dry sagebrush and whistled down barren slopes, its howls matching the cries of anguish loosed by Sun Valley employees over the lack of snow.

"I had a truck to go over to Proctor," William Castagnetto reminisced, "and I followed the boys back and forth to work. It would whip up the dust, and it was so dusty on the road clear to December that they all called it the Ketchum Con. We never had a drop of moisture from the first day we started, the twenty-sixth of August. Not a drop of moisture of any kind, not a flake of snow, until the fourteenth of December."

On December 14 it snowed. By six o'clock that even-

Soup Xerxes, Pheasant Under Glass

. . . the Ritz in the Wilderness

ing it had snowed an inch, and the storm continued through the night.

The previous December at the same time, there had been thirteen inches of snow on the ground at Ketchum. The eighteen-year average for December was sixteen inches.

But as the date of the grand opening—December 21—drew near, a couple of inches was still all Sun Valley had. There was nothing to do but to go ahead with the opening. Harriman was in New York City, attending the debut of his daughter Mary, so it fell to William Jeffers, President of the Union Pacific, to host the gala affair. The stars poured into Sun Valley. They were greeted by Raymond Stevens, the first manager of the Sun Valley Lodge, who tried to direct their attention away from the lack of snow.

The lodge itself was a most helpful distraction. Its actual cost had topped Steve Hannagan's suggested million-dollar mark and gone to a million and a half. Accommodations included elevator service, an x-ray equipped physician and surgeon department, barber shop, bachelor's lounge, writing rooms, and valet service. Carved accents heightened the rustic ambience of the main lounge on the second floor: two eagles and an owl stared down at the guests, while the guests in turn could gaze through huge glass windows at the skating rink below.

The doors off the lodge's long corridors opened into rooms finished in redwood or oak with copper fittings and furnished with overstuffed furniture done in red or green. Perhaps small by later hotel standards, the guest rooms were lavish for 1936—especially considering their near-wilderness location. And so that the moneyed easterners wouldn't feel completely cut off from civilization, Harriman had induced Saks Fifth Avenue to open a shop in the lodge.

But while the lodge had all the comforts of one of New York's finest, the thing the guests had traveled so far for and heard so much about—that deep Sun Valley powder—was still missing when they awoke on the morning of the grand opening. Threatening clouds hung over the Sawtooths, but instead of dumping snow on Sun Valley, they poured rain.

That evening, William Jeffers presided over the opening banquet. The menu included Manhattan cocktail, *brioche au caviar*, beef tea *des viveurs*, *paillettes dorées*, *suprêmes* of sole *au champagne valley lodge*, *tournedos sautés chatelaine*, *pommes mascotte*, *haricots verts fins au gratin*, *salade des îsles*, *ananas surprise*, and Union Pacific *frivolités americaines*. The guests enjoyed fine hock and champagne, and the meal ended with *café des princes*, cigars and liqueurs.

After dinner, the crowd danced to the music of New York City's Harl Smith, who'd been brought in especially for the affair. (He ended up staying around Sun Valley for some time as one of its orchestra leaders.)

At eleven o'clock that night, radio station KSL of Salt Lake City provided a live broadcast from the lodge, with Jeffers, Schaffgotsch, Stevens, and several others giving short speeches.

Lodge dining room

Lodge kitchen

Two days after the banquet the *Idaho Statesman* carried the following post-grand-opening story:

"Still echoing with the music and laughter of the opening banquet and dance Monday night, Sun Valley Lodge spent a comparatively quiet Tuesday as prominent Idahoans, guests of the new million and a half dollar resort at the formal opening, departed by the carload for their homes.

"Guests from the East wandered about the resort and inspected all its recreational possibilities, unpacked bags overlooked in the rush and excitement of the opening night festivities, and prepared to settle down and enjoy their stay in Ketchum.

"The absence of snow was a disappointment to ski enthusiasts, but Tuesday afternoon Count Felix Schaffgotsch, lodge ski master, arranged a trip in one of the news buses, and some of the guests donned their ski outfits and drove to Galena Summit, where there was enough snow to make a slide possible.

"Other guests went horseback riding, drove around to inspect the surrounding country, or rode up and down on the ski lifts, descending from the moving chairs on the tops of Proctor and Dollar Mountains to get the best possible view of the magnificent scenery afforded by the towering Sawtooths.

"The day was warm and several of the visitors swam in the outdoor pool, which is heated to a temperature of 80 degrees, making comfortable swimming possible even in nippy weather. Lodge employees worked on the outdoor skating rink, installing flood lights and a loud

Attention to every detail

"Bavarians" provide skating music

Music makers

Getting the rhythm

speaker system which will furnish skaters with music for waltzing on ice.

"Some of the women played bridge in the beautifully furnished main lounge, and the smack of paddles on ping pong balls was audible all afternoon from the game room, which is equipped for backgammon, checkers, card games of all sorts and descriptions, with a ping pong table at the back of the room.

"Lodge employees and officials were busy preparing for the influx of guests with reservations for the last of December and New Year's Eve."

On December 27, snow began falling at Sun Valley and five inches soon collected on Dollar and Proctor mountains. The sighs of relief were, however, premature. By this time Averell Harriman had arrived from New York, and he and the staff soon saw that they had made one crucial mistake. The ski hills looked like they were covered by a day-old beard.

"It was largely our fault that we didn't cut the sagebrush down," said Harriman. "We expected it to be covered."

But Harriman didn't let the near-snowless slopes spoil the fun. "The house was filled, and everybody was excited, but you just couldn't ski," he said. "So we didn't charge them for their board and lodging for the three or four days there was no snow, which made them very happy and made them stay on."

In fact, the lack of snow may have made for better publicity than if the guests had been greeted with a blizzard on opening day. An incident in New York made Harriman feel the snowless conditions might not hurt. White Face, a skiing area in that state, had been developed on the wrong side of the mountain, where the runs were very icy. Harriman stepped in and developed the other side, where the skiing was better.

"I went up the lift with a man who was in charge of the construction, an engineer who was going to run the place," Harriman recalled. On the way up, the lift broke down and the two men were stranded for some time. "He said to me, 'Isn't this terrible for opening day?' and I said 'No, we'll get as much publicity from this.' Sure enough, my picture with the engineer was taken and shown all over the United States. And the fact that we didn't have any snow at Sun Valley gave us twice the publicity we could have had with it."

Sun Valley did get the publicity, but chances are it was more because of the class of people who were forced to spend their time in such idle pursuits as playing checkers or reading books while they waited for the snow. There was, for example, the film company waiting to shoot the winter sports sequences for "I Met Him in Paris," starring Claudette Colbert, Robert Young, and Melvyn Douglas.

Colbert stayed over for New Year's Eve and was joined by a crush of Hollywood stars, including Lily Damita, Errol Flynn, Joan Bennett, and Madeleine Carroll. They were all guests at the second big party scheduled for Sun Valley—the New Year's bash. That night, while the *beau monde* celebrated, it snowed. The world outside the lodge turned white, and by morning

Galena Summit, north of Sun Valley

Relaxing in the lodge pool

there was nearly two feet of snow on the ground and the sagebrush was covered. But the main concern December 31 wasn't snow, but party.

Before dancing, the guests enjoyed another exotic menu prepared by Sun Valley's French chefs. The dinner, served by waiters in full tuxedos, consisted of *canapés muscovites,* green turtle soup *au Xerxes,* celery, almonds, olives, *mousselin* of lobster *polignac,* breast of chicken *inedité, gauffrettes,* peas *à la française,* and salad. The finale was a flaming plum pudding.

The clubrooms and dance floors were packed until five in the morning. Claudette Colbert was having an exceptionally good time, until a Chicago banker, C.F. Glore, came to her table and asked her to dance. Colbert was sitting with Joan Bennett and movie producer David O. Selznick. Somebody—reportedly Selznick—objected to Glore's invitation to Colbert and promptly slugged the Chicago man. The *New York Herald Tribune's* headline the next day read "Sun Valley Opens With A Bang."

Lloyd Castagnetto was a student that year, but he was at the party. "I wore my first tuxedo, and I had the time of my life," he recalled. "If I remember correctly, that was when a couple of Hollywood producers got involved with a man who was partially inebriated—a very influential man from back east. There was blood all over everything that night."

Although news reports pointed the punch at Selznick, Castagnetto thought the man who did the damage was the dashing Errol Flynn.

Snow at last—Claudette Colbert (r.)

Robert Young readies for a day on the slopes

"I didn't see what happened originally, but there was fisticuffs. He thought the man was out of line, and there was some punches. They calmed it down and the party went on, as far as that's concerned. But it was certainly something that marred the festivities for the evening."

The Selznick-Flynn escapade faded from everyone's memory quickly enough, and Sun Valley settled into the routine of a winter sports resort. Railroad passengers going to the valley usually went as far as Shoshone, where they were met by sleighs or buses that would transport them to the lodge. There they were greeted with music by one of the Sun Valley bands, flowers in their rooms, and (if they were important enough) champagne. Sun Valley guests, in short, were spoiled rotten.

Yet it was a peaceful sort of place. If anyone had a taste for violence, he could amble on down to the cowboy bars that lined Ketchum's streets. There was always someone there to oblige. After all, Ketchum was a western town in the fullest sense, and the construction of a ski resort which brought crowds of fashionable tourists also brought hordes of weather-beaten, whiskey-drinking cowboys—young and old.

"They were not unfriendly; it wasn't the red-neck kind of thing where they disliked the outsider," said one longtime Sun Valley resident. "I didn't see that at all. Fighting, yes. There were lots of fights and there was a lot of booze and there were some very tough characters. And there were certain people that you knew would always fight."

It wasn't that the "tough characters" singled out Sun

Starlets filming "I Met Him in Paris" take a ski break

Valley guests. When the time came to let off steam, "they'd pick on anybody. There was some resentment though—sort of 'these new people are coming in here and jazzing up our life.' Sort of the feeling that Idaho has now about the Californians."

Sun Valley seemed like a stage to the rest of the nation. There were pictures in *Life Magazine* of writer Claude Binyon wallowing helplessly on skis, Lydia Du Pont of the Delaware Du Ponts sitting in the lodge talking over her day's skiing, and Averell Harriman and his wife Marie dozing outside a ski hut, soaking up the hot Idaho sun in March.

To America, Sun Valley meant glamour—pictures in the papers and stories of fun and excitement in the sun.

To certain elements in Ketchum, Sun Valley meant money.

Idaho in the 1930's put legalized gambling on a local option basis. The Ketchum area chose to allow it, which was not really unusual in the state. Even in conservative Boise, Idaho's Republican-dominated capital and largest population center (in the late thirties Boise residents numbered fewer than 30,000), clubs like the Buffalo and the Havana offered gaming. If straightlaced Boise, with its large Mormon population, could allow gambling—from roulette and twenty-one to the more innocent but popular slot machines—then Ketchum, with its influx of moneyed movie stars and business tycoons, could certainly stand whatever evils Lady Luck brought with her.

Gambling was confined to Ketchum and to Hailey,

Mrs. Harriman starts the teams in the first annual Dog Derby

Skiers leaving lodge for the lifts

Sun Valley's finest cutter

Fresh powder and free as the wind

eleven miles from Ketchum. Asked why there was no gambling in Sun Valley itself, an idea which would have seemed natural, a former employee responded, "You mean on Union Pacific property?"

Union Pacific wanted no part of the gambling, and so when Gary Cooper or Clark Gable or Ernest Hemingway wanted to pass the time at the gaming tables, he wandered down to the Casino or Alpine or Sawtooth or

Basking in the sun

Still the "wild west"—Ketchum casino

106

Tram to mingle with the locals. In the 1960's and 1970's, Sun Valley no longer needed gambling to lure people to its slopes. But in 1937 and 1938, there were numerous Sun Valley visitors who went to the resort not to ski but to escape the crush of Hollywood crowds or the press of the business world. Gambling was as much a pastime for some as skiing was for others.

Jack Hemingway was just out of high school when he joined his father for a stay in Sun Valley. Gambling was alive and well when he first arrived in the Ketchum area. "There were good things about it and there were bad things," Jack remembers.

One of the bad things he remembers involved a Hollywood producer named Mark Hellinger, who was in Sun Valley to negotiate with Ernest Hemingway over the rights to some of his material. "He came up and they made a very big money deal, for a bunch of short stories of my father's which were to be made into movies over a period of years," said Hemingway. "The deal was made and the agreement was signed."

Before the ink on the contract had dried, Hellinger was headed for Ketchum for a few drinks and a game of cards. Hellinger was a rather sickly man, and his choice of establishments was as poor as his health. He picked the Thunderbird, Ketchum's least outstanding bar.

"He got smashed and lost a bunch of money," said Jack. "When they found he didn't have enough money for a cab home, they wouldn't give him any; they just threw him out."

By the time Hellinger reached Sun Valley, tramping through the mud and snow along the ribbon of road connecting the resort with Ketchum, he was violently ill. "I guess he got pneumonia, and it was within a few weeks that he died," Hemingway said. "His widow immediately contacted my father."

Hellinger's widow asked Ernest Hemingway if he would return the earnest money—somewhere in the neighborhood of $50,000—because it was needed to

Rustic gambling spot

107

clear up her husband's debts. Hemingway returned it immediately.

"So there were bad things about it," Jack continued. "I'd say in any of the places on Main Street, that sort of thing would never happen. I mean, if some guy were down to his last dime, somebody would have staked him to a ride home somewhere along the line."

The Hellinger incident was an isolated one. The stars and other Sun Valley guests continued to flock to downtown Ketchum to try their hands at cards and the spin of the roulette wheel. It was only natural that, with Sun Valley's fame spreading, somebody would decide it was prime territory for a plush gambling casino.

In the late 1930's a huge, bald-headed man named Dutch Weinbrenner appeared at Sun Valley to look over the area. Not too long after that, construction began on the Christiana, a very "up-town" dinner club that brought a touch of class to gambling in Ketchum.

Weinbrenner was a big man, over six feet tall, and there were worried whispers throughout Ketchum and Sun Valley that mob money was financing the Christiana. Weinbrenner, the tongues wagged, was a member of Detroit's notorious Purple Gang. While it is now generally conceded that Weinbrenner did indeed have a mob background, he must have left his gun and brass knuckles in Detroit. He settled into the routine of overlord of the luxurious restaurant, and if any of his Detroit pals visited him, they did it in the most respectable way.

Weinbrenner had investigated both Las Vegas and Ketchum as possible locations for his restaurant. But in 1938, Las Vegas was a small, nondescript town in the snake-infested Nevada desert, while Ketchum seemed ideal, the retreat of the rich and famous.

Don and Gretchen Fraser came to Sun Valley in 1937. They remember the Christiana as the place where everybody went, "a beautiful stone place where you ate marvelous food.

"And Darryl Zanuck used to spend a lot of time there," Don Fraser said. "And then later on, Marilyn Monroe and people like that, major writers, would come in."

To Don, Weinbrenner seemed more like a grandfather type than a mobster. "He was a really down-to-earth man; he didn't enter into any social activities at all." But Weinbrenner did keep irregular hours. "I would go down to meet the train early in the morning. I'd be down in the lobby about six or seven o'clock, and lots of times I'd see Dutch just coming in. He'd always be pretty well loaded. When he left the Christiana down there he'd always take his teeth out and put them in his pocket. I always enjoyed talking to him in the morning for a few minutes."

When Weinbrenner died, his sons came out from Detroit to take him home for burial. The Christiana was torn down and another establishment of the same name, but owned by different people, was built across the street.

Gambling eventually died also. In the early 1950's a crusade was started, and Idaho law enforcement officers

A popular pastime

Santa and the reindeer

staged raids and busted down doors to search out places where gambling dens still operated. But in the late 1930's, the tables and wheels and one-armed bandits helped breathe new life into Ketchum; the clubs on Main Street were filled at night with cowboys and Sun Valley guests intent on making their stay in the small mountain village as exciting as possible.

Time swept by. Sun Valley's first season had been a success, and so was its second. To help inaugurate the second season, Harriman and a group of friends rode the Union Pacific's new diesel streamliner "City of Los Angeles" from New York to Shoshone. In addition to Harriman and his wife, passengers included Mr. and Mrs. C.L. May of Beverly Hills, publisher Harold Ginsberg of Viking Press, and William Jeffers. Hungry for news of what the elite and rich were doing at Sun Valley, the nation accompanied Harriman across the country vicariously through Associated Press dispatches.

The train arrived in Sun Valley on December 20, just in time for the opening ceremonies. Two bands, Bus Vaughn from the Sun Valley Lodge and Harl Smith, borrowed from the Christiana, welcomed Harriman and his guests at the Ketchum station.

The official opening was concluded that night, with KSL once again broadcasting the events live. Harriman addressed the assembled, as did Idaho's governor, Barzilla Clark; Bill Jeffers; Felix Schaffgotsch; Hans Hauser, head of the Sun Valley Ski School; and Ah Sook, an Eskimo reindeer specialist.

It would no doubt be interesting to know what the speakers said—especially Ah Sook—but unfortunately none of the words were recorded for posterity. More unfortunately for Sook, his job didn't last very long. He had been brought to Sun Valley to tend a herd of reindeer imported to give the place a high-mountain look. But the reindeer grew sick, developed pinkeye, and were soon snapping at children who tried to pet them. They became a source of embarrassment to the resort and soon disappeared. So did Ah Sook.

Those who heard the speeches on radio, or read the reports carried in the newspapers across the country, could only envy what they were missing. In that remote Idaho village, Austrian ski instructors were singing rousing drinking songs, and from the Ram, a quaint bar and restaurant in the Challenger Inn, came the strains of a Bavarian orchestra. The day ended with dancing at the Ram and the Duchin Room in the lodge.

Despite the lack of snow at the start, Sun Valley had survived its first season. The way its second season began seemed to indicate that the cowboys, railroad presidents, European ski masters, and local shopkeepers had found themselves a good thing.

Instructor Friedl Pfeifer creates his own snowstorm

Averell Harriman had brought the European ski resort to America. He had introduced the chairlift and built the million-dollar lodge, and he had made America sit up and take notice of a part of the West that might otherwise have remained a sheep-grazing land on the edge of a dying frontier town.

When Sun Valley opened, there was just one more thing Averell Harriman had to have to make sure the resort would become more than just a meeting place for the rich and famous. He needed somebody to teach those people how to ski—the right way to ski, the way they skied in Europe. What Harriman needed were some genuine Austrian ski instructors, the kind whose manner and speech would add authentic European elegance to his playground.

So while the lodge was being built, the ski runs shaped, and the chairlift invented, Harriman sent scouts to Europe to bring those ski instructors back to the U.S.A. He was not so much submitting to a popular snobbery as facing the facts. In 1936 skiing was in its infancy in America; Scandinavians who had settled in the Pacific Northwest (or so the story goes) sent sons to schools in the East, notably to Dartmouth, and those sons introduced the sport there. Still, there were few people in the States who knew skiing well enough to teach it. In Austria, however, the grand guru of downhill skiing, Hans Schneider, had been molding teachers for many years. Using the Arlberg method, Schneider was taking young backwoods farmers and turning them into smooth-talking ski instructors.

Idaho's Austrians

. . . "Bend Zee Knees!"

The "lonely life" in the Idaho wilderness

114

Learning to "cut the flag"—Hans Hauser instructing

Sun Valley's Austrian ski instructors—and the first group was entirely Austrian—would become as much a part of the resort as the snow. Some won the hearts of the women they taught, rousing envy in the men who watched them, marrying into money or into sorrow, leaving behind happy or tragic stories. Some didn't leave, but settled into the Sun Valley population, oddities of sorts, with their staccato speech, to the transient tourists.

The most durable of them has proved to be Sigi Engl, who became head of the ski school in 1952. Like many of the Sun Valley instructors, Engl came from Kitzbühel. He has stayed the longest and spends all his time in the Valley.

An expert run on Baldy

There are three cottages near the lodge. One belongs to Averell Harriman, and one of the others to Engl. Sigi has been one of the most popular party guests in Sun Valley, whether the affair is thrown by current owner Bill Janss or by movie producer ("Funny Girl," "Robin and Marian") Ray Stark.

Engl forged close personal ties with many of the stars he taught, and became known as Gary Cooper's private ski instructor. When he first went to Sun Valley, Cooper had little desire to ski. But eventually his wife Rocky and daughter Maria pushed him into it. "They nagged him to death so he just started. He skied all around here," Engl commented. Cooper had a bad leg, and while filming movies he had to mount his horse from a certain angle to keep from looking clumsy. It didn't cramp his style on the slopes, however; he skied beautifully.

Jimmy Stewart, on the other hand, had such bad knees that he was prevented from taking up skiing as anything more than a very now-and-again thing. Engl calls actress Janet Leigh the best skier among the Hollywood set, Betty Hutton the worst.

While Hutton may have seemed a bad skier to Sigi Engl, she was the favorite pupil of another Austrian instructor, Sepp Froehlich. "In the old days you tried to tell the people how if they fell down to get up," said Froehlich. "Teaching modern skiing, it's not that way anymore. You cut this all out now. But one day I said 'Betty, now you should fall down so I can show you how to get up.' And she told me, 'Sepp, I never fall down.'

Ingrid Bergman and friends

117

Gary Cooper leads Sigi Engl and Clark Gable down the hill

118

So I told myself, 'Oh, I show you you will fall down.' I made a track from the back slope out in the deep snow, so she went down. I start laughing at her, you know, and I say 'Betty, I thought you never fall down!'"

When the Hollywood crowd descended on Sun Valley, it was natural that some of them would be more enchanted by the place than others. Clark Gable came occasionally, but didn't become a regular. Ingrid Bergman, Fred MacMurray, Ray Milland, and countless other stars spent time at Sun Valley and moved on. Others became habitués. Darryl Zanuck, one of Hollywood's most powerful men and a founder of 20th Century Fox, was a steady customer and a familiar sight on the mountains.

So was the widowed Norma Shearer, who returned to Sun Valley winter and summer and was one of the first to be swept off her feet by a ski instructor, sweeping him off in turn to a home in Beverly Hills. By 1939, Sun Valley had become something of a summer draw, with horseback riding facilities, a nine-hole golf course, and tennis courts. Shearer could be seen playing tennis or riding her bicycle about the manicured grounds. She could also be seen quite a bit, winter and summer, with Marty Arrouge. Arrouge wasn't Austrian, but Basque. They were married in 1939 in a simple ceremony at Sun Valley.

The couple's best man was Otto Lang, who would later become head of Sun Valley's ski school and still later an internationally known movie producer. "It's certainly been a durable marriage," said Lang of the

Norma Shearer

Kaare Engen airborne

Shearer/Arrouge match. "I mean, they've been wonderful to each other."

Another instructor's brush with Hollywood didn't turn out quite so well. Ragnar Qvale's was a classic tale of discovery and abandonment: a powerful Hollywood talent scout finds a handsome young man and offers him a chance for a screen test. According to the *Idaho Statesman*, Qvale's discovery went like this:

"A Norwegian immigrant boy's determination to master the English language when he came here from Trondheim, Norway, 10 years ago Tuesday won him a screen test and a chance for Hollywood fame and fortune. He is Ragnar Qvale, 21, Sun Valley's handsomest ski instructor, who is now on his way to Hollywood with Darryl Zanuck, chief executive of Twentieth Century Fox Films, who offered Qvale his chance while vacationing at this famous winter resort.

"Qvale, a graduate of the University of Washington, said that while he was eating dinner in the Ram, Sun Valley's continental cafe, the other night, Zanuck came over to the table and after a lengthy conversation asked him if he would like a screen test. 'That's all there was to it,' the tall, blond, evenly-featured boy said.

"'I think the one thing that impressed Mr. Zanuck,' he continued, 'was my knowledge of English. When I came to America I didn't know a word of it, but I made a point of picking it up. Now I speak it a lot better than some people who were born here.' While at college, Qvale studied architecture and was an outstanding member of the Husky ski team. He was given his appointment to the staff of the Sun Valley Ski School as a result of placing third in last year's Combined Four Events Intercollegiate Ski Meet and sixth in the jump event of the Sun Valley Open last spring.

"His only dramatic experience was acquired in high school, he said. 'I think Mr. Zanuck's offer is swell, but confidentially I expect to be back teaching skiing in a week.'"

Darryl Zanuck, his son Dick, and Otto Lang

Session on the slopes

The newspaper ran a picture of Qvale overseeing Zanuck tucked in a tight snowplow, and the caption beneath it said he was urging the Hollywood mogul to "bend zee knees." In a few days, the paper said, the roles will be reversed and Zanuck will be urging Qvale to "open zee eyes."

Unfortunately for Qvale, he apparently didn't "open zee eyes" enough, because he went to Hollywood, took the screen test, and was never heard from again.

Otto Lang's story is a happier one. Lang came to America from Austria in 1936 to open a ski school at Mount Rainier in Washington. He would later start two more schools, at Mount Baker and Mount Hood, in Oregon.

Lang had his first taste of movie-making in Oregon. Sonja Henie, the Norwegian skating heroine of the 1936 Olympics, was filming "Thin Ice" with Tyrone Power at Mount Baker. As an expert skier and veteran of countless winter sports activities, Lang was asked to be technical advisor. Later, at Mount Rainier, Lang did a film called "Snow Flight," which was an instructional documentary on skiing. "I appeared in front of the camera demonstrating skiing, and I also helped with the technical end of it," he recalled. "You know, finding the shots and setting up the cameras."

"Snow Flight" opened at New York's Radio City Music Hall, sharing the screen with a cartoon feature. "It was probably the first ski picture ever shown on the screen anywhere," Lang believes.

The story is that Lang made the move to Sun Valley

Otto Lang

Sigi Engl

in 1939 because of the interest taken in him by Nelson Rockefeller. Rockefeller had attended the Mount Rainier school and had liked Lang so much that every time he went to Sun Valley he asked Friedl Pfeifer, head of the ski school, why he didn't bring Otto Lang to Idaho. Pfeifer, an old Austrian colleague of Lang's (both were from St. Anton and had taught together there), finally did.

Lang took over the ski school in 1942, just in time for Sun Valley to shut down for World War II, when it served as a naval hospital. When it reopened in 1946, Lang was there, ready to head the school again. But during the war Lang was, in his words, "really into the film business," making military training films and documentaries.

Later, in 1952, Lang helped make the movie credited with establishing Sun Valley's reputation in Europe. "I was deeply involved with 'Sun Valley Serenade,'" said Lang. "I shot all the exteriors and was very close to Darryl Zanuck. Then Zanuck took me under his wing; he said, 'Why don't you come to Hollywood?' and that's the way it started."

But Lang had actually been involved in an ambitious filmmaking schedule before the invitation from Zanuck. "I worked at the studios in the summertime," Lang said, "and then in the winter I would return to Sun Valley. Eventually I realized I had to do one or the other. When I had an opportunity to produce a few big pictures, I took the chance."

Lang went to Hollywood and soon began producing some of the industry's most respected films, including "Five Fingers," "Call Northside 777," and "White Witch Doctor." In addition, his documentaries have been nominated four times for academy awards.

Lang's Sun Valley experiences proved to be valuable to his career in the movie industry. "It was a good, very wonderful thing, because you met such a tremendous cross section of people," he said. "You had an opportunity to get close to them on the ski slopes, and many a career emerged from that."

When World War II broke out, many of the Austrian ski instructors were confronted with a dilemma most of them never dreamed they'd face when they left Europe for steady work in America. Jeanne Cutaia, a stenographer for Sun Valley, was helping prepare for the opening of the resort's sixth season. She remembers December 7, 1941, very well. "I was walking across between the lodge and the [Challenger] Inn and it was the slow season, they weren't open yet. I walked into the Challenger lobby and the radio was on, and I listened to it for a minute. Everybody had this startled, horrible look on their face. I just couldn't believe it."

The ski instructors were just as surprised and shocked. "Most of them were pretty non-political in this country," said Cutaia. "They didn't mingle in politics."

In fact, what Hitler had been doing in Europe was but a distant rumor to those enclosed in the snowy world of Sun Valley. "We were so isolated, it was like we were off on an island," Cutaia said. "You had very little in the way of information. Unless you happened to pick up

Sun Valley

Sun Valley's Main Street, the Ram and the Challenger

Instructors Hans Hauser, Roland Cossman, Joe Bednedeckter, Franz Epp, Ive Schweighayes, Al Dingl

an outside newspaper and look at it, you didn't know anything that was going on in the outside world. And we *called* it 'the outside world.'"

If the residents of Sun Valley, all caught up in their tidy little existence of skiing and partying and living something of a wealthy recluse's life, weren't aware of the world outside, that certainly didn't mean the world was not aware of them. Of course, the press the resort received included stories on the Austrian ski instructors. And it wasn't very long before an agency of that outside world—the Federal Bureau of Investigation—found its way to the valley to talk to some of those instructors and some of the other European help.

Frederic Blechmann had been living in London when, on the advice of his father, he decided to come to America instead of returning to his German homeland.

Count Felix and Hans Hauser

128

He settled in New York City, where his brothers were living, and went to work in a hotel. It was here that some of Harriman's men, on a talent search for Europeans with hotel experience, found him and lured him to Idaho. Blechmann arrived in Sun Valley in 1937 and became a waiter, then a captain, in room service.

Like the ski instructors, Blechmann still had ties in Europe—family, friends, and a sense of personal belonging. But the Sun Valley "foreigners" were by no means a band of Hitler spies. Still, the rumors flew thicker than a mountain blizzard. Blechmann, who eventually became maître d' in the lodge dining room, is philosophical about the gossip: "War is war," he said. "Don't forget, anytime we have war, whether it's here in this country or in Austria, Germany, France, or England, you are being watched if you are a foreigner. People talk about you and so on."

One night soon after war was declared, the FBI moved in on the Austrian ski instructors—and Blechmann. Hans Hauser, Sepp Froehlich, and Friedl Pfeifer, who was director of the ski school at the time, were arrested with Blechmann and, as Blechmann put it, "We were all put in the clink for a few days in Hailey."

From Hailey, the men were taken to Salt Lake City. One Austrian ski instructor who wasn't arrested, Walt Prager, found the whole thing a bit ludicrous. His thoughts are recorded in John Jay's *Ski Down Through the Years:*

"They were so harmless, those guys . . . they were schkiers, not schpies. . . . Yah, I had to laugh when they arrested Hauser and Froehlich and Pfeifer and all those Austrians, you know, for supposed subversive activities and schpying, they would have been caught . . . the first second they would have been caught. . . . I had to laugh. Hauser had about four times as much money in the bank in Hailey as his total salary, which he got from tips for his schkiing . . . and the government wanted to know where it all came from and he wouldn't tell them. . . . So they schtuck him in a concentration camp or an internment camp or whatever they called them. . . . They thought he was a paid agent, with all this money. Yah, these guys were talking about Hitler and how fantastic everything is in Germany and so on. . . . They hadn't been here too long and they were impressed by the whole thing . . . and the FBI was sitting around there listening to these boys and they thought, 'Oh boy, we got something big here' . . . and so one morning they arrested them at four o'clock in the morning and took them all off to jail. . . . You know Sepp Froehlich? They were all in the Salt Lake City jail together. . . . You have never seen anything so funny! Froehlich, he was having a great big chaise lounge in his cell . . . all his wealth came from the Utah Hotel . . . a bottle of wine for breakfast and champagne for lunch . . . and Friedl Pfeifer was next door getting the same treatment. . . . He was married to the owner of the hotel. . . . And then they were released. . . . They had a choice of going to concentration camp or into the army, and Hauser elected concentration camp. . . . He

Fresh powder

was in the Dakotas. . . . But Friedl and the rest of the boys said, 'Sure, we go in the army,' and a lot of them wound up in the 10th Mountain [Division]. . . ."

Prager wasn't fantasizing on the Austrians' relatively luxurious existence in the Salt Lake City jail. Froehlich's and Pfeifer's wives followed their spouses to Salt Lake and lived near their husbands during their detention. "We didn't really suffer," said Blechmann. Still, each day brought new uncertainties. "Of course, you went through all these investigations, and you had to face a board one day—of all the very great citizens of Salt Lake City." The board would ask questions. And then more questions. "They asked about the past," said Blechmann; "why did you come over, and so on. To be frank, they [the instructors] were all farm kids, mostly. They came over here and got caught up in the maelstrom."

After two and a half months of investigating, the FBI decided their "schpies" were nothing more than they seemed—three robust, pink-cheeked ski instructors and one waiter. They were released and, as Prager noted, given the options of joining the American army or spending the war in a detention camp. All but Hauser chose military service. Blechmann went to the South Pacific, while the others—Froehlich and Pfeifer—joined the legendary 10th Mountain Division.

Froehlich feels no bitterness about his treatment during the war. "I was treated well," he said. "I have no complaints. I was released and then I just volunteered for the army. I knew that if I wanted to stay in the

Hans Hauser

country, I should do the job."

After the war, most of the instructors returned to skiing, or the ski world. Sigi Engl, who had also opted to go to war against his homeland, eventually took control of the Sun Valley Ski School. Sepp Froehlich drifted back, along with another veteran instructor, Andy Henning. Friedl Pfeifer became a rancher in Montana.

Hans Hauser, who alone had chosen detention instead of the army, was finally released from the Dakota camp. He returned to Sun Valley to act out a real-life drama that had all the elements of a 1940's B-movie script.

Hauser, who won the Austrian ski championship in 1933 and 1934, had been selected by Harriman as the first director of the Sun Valley ski school. A likable man, with chiseled good looks, he had led the idyllic life of any instructor in the valley in the 1930's— teaching Hollywood's loveliest and strongest the art of skiing during the day and attending parties at night in the always lively lodge. But after the war, Hauser had the misfortune to fall in love. The light of his life was Virginia Hill, one-time girlfriend of mobster Bugsy Siegel.

"At heart, Virginia Hill was a very good woman," Otto Lang recalled. "She had a golden heart and was very sentimental. Of course, she was mixed up with all these people, Bugsy Siegel and the underworld element, and of course that made it very tough. And it remains a mystery today what her stranglehold was— you know, what she knew that forced Siegel to support

Back Pay Gulch

132

Skeeplechasing, Hans Hauser

her. This has never been solved, this mystery. But there was nothing evil about Virginia. And Hans Hauser was a very decent fellow, a good Joe.''

After Bugsy Siegel was murdered in her apartment, Virginia Hill had fled to Sun Valley, where she took up residence among the whispering of the lodge's young staff. And whatever hold she had on Siegel, it remained after his death—somebody from outside the resort was supporting her. Once a week, the rumor went, Virginia Hill would receive a shoebox from somebody, and every week the curiosity of the help sharpened. Finally one day, the bellboy in charge of delivering the shoebox dropped it "accidentally." The string broke and, the story goes, hundred-dollar bills spilled onto the floor.

Whether the shoebox story is true or the final figment of frustrated imaginations is uncertain. But the fact is that Virginia Hill "always paid everything in hundred-dollar bills," according to Don Fraser. "And sometimes she'd tip a bellboy that much."

As his love affair with Virginia Hill deepened, Hauser sought advice from his good friend Otto Lang. Lang remembers one particular conversation. "He said he wanted to get married to Virginia Hill, and I said 'Hans, this is all fine and good but do you realize what the consequences would be? You'd be cutting yourself off from all your friends and socially you couldn't be moving around with Virginia due to her background and everything, and it would be a very difficult situation. You must be aware of it.' I talked to him till about two o'clock in the night, and he said 'You are right, Otto, you are absolutely right. I've decided I'm not going to get married.' And he blessed me."

Otto Lang went to sleep worry-free. The next morning he awoke, dressed, and left for the daily meeting with the other ski instructors. "I got to the meeting-place and they said, 'Do you know what happened?' And I say, 'No, what happened?' And they said, 'Hans Hauser eloped with Virginia; they've gone.'"

Felix Schaffgotsch

Hans Hauser had indeed eloped with Virginia Hill. From that moment on, his life was never the same. Virginia eventually got into trouble with the crime-fighting Kefauver Senate Committee over her connections with organized crime. Later, problems with income tax arose—evidently the shoeboxes were not declared—and the two of them were forced to flee the country. Virginia and Hans traveled to Chile and then to his native Austria. Although they settled outside Salzburg near Hans's brother Max, things apparently went from bad to worse. Virginia Hill eventually died a rather mysterious death by poisoning, and in 1974 Hans Hauser hanged himself.

As for Count Felix Schaffgotsch, the man who blazed the trail for the Austrian ski instructors, he was never to return to the slopes of Idaho. It was never clear whether Schaffgotsch joined the German army voluntarily or whether, as an Austrian, he was forced into joining Hitler's troops against his will. In any event, he died in battle fighting for the Third Reich, on the snow-covered Russian Front. Ironically, Averell Harriman was Ambassador to Russia when Schaffgotsch fell.

Ernest Hemingway

There are two things, it is said, that put Sun Valley on the international map. The first was the movie "Sun Valley Serenade," which spread the resort visually through America and then the world.

The second was the choice of the Valley as a favored retreat by Ernest Hemingway, the forceful literary master of the strong and honest quests in life. If Ernest Hemingway, towering author that he was, chose Sun Valley to hunt, to shoot pheasant, and to swap jokes and tales with Gary Cooper, then there must (reasoned the world) be something special about the place.

For years, Hemingway had spent time on the El Barte Ranch in Wyoming, and had grown to love the rugged country of that state and of neighboring Montana. A couple of early Sun Valley employees, Lloyd Arnold and Gene Van Guilder, heard about Hemingway's fascination with the ranch and, thinking about the publicity which might be reaped if he changed to Sun Valley, suggested that somebody should try to lure Hemingway to Idaho. The notion was mentioned to the redoubtable Steve Hannagan, who seemed to have a way of arranging just about anything. Hannagan knew that Hemingway was currently engrossed in the turbulent Spanish Civil War and might not be interested in moving anyplace, especially to a new resort in the Wild West; but Steve was never one to let a good idea drop. Hannagan knew a man in Key West, where Hemingway often retreated to write, who, he said, might be able to approach the author about the idea in the future.

Two years later, in 1939, a big, rugged man, dressed

He Loved the Fall

. . . Hemingway's Sun Valley

Tillie and Lloyd Arnold

in levis, studded belt, plain workshirt and a leather vest, showed up at Sun Valley. It was Ernest Hemingway. With him was Martha Gellhorn, who wrote *The Trouble I've Seen* and would later become Hemingway's third wife.

Arnold and Van Guilder proudly took their new arrivals to the lodge, where a startled Pat Rogers ordered them put into the resort's best rooms.

The mystery of Hemingway's sudden appearance at Sun Valley was partly explained by Hannagan, who reported to Arnold and Van Guilder that Hemingway had indeed been approached about staying in Sun Valley. Although the writer hadn't made any commitment, he'd mentioned that he might stop by on his way to Montana, to see what the lay of the land was like.

Hemingway liked the lay of the land; he immediately

became fast friends with Lloyd and Tillie Arnold and Gene Van Guilder; and he was especially entranced by Idaho's bird hunting possibilities. Game bird shooting in Hemingway's Montana stomping grounds was very limited.

So Ernest and Martha plopped down in the Sun Valley Lodge's finest suite—at a special rate, which bordered on camping in for free—and stayed, and stayed, and stayed. Hemingway became fascinated with Sun Valley and Ketchum, taking to the hills, stomping through the sagebrush, and loving every minute of it.

He stayed in room 206, a room that has become immortalized—partly through a strong publicity push by Sun Valley itself—as the place where he wrote *For Whom the Bell Tolls*. Since everything about Sun Valley borders on the make-believe, it's not too surprising that, according to Jack Hemingway, the story of his father standing at his typewriter in room 206, pounding out *For Whom the Bell Tolls*, is about half fable.

Much of the book had been written before Hemingway piloted his big black Buick to Sun Valley. But still, Jack said, there was a great deal of work to be done. Hemingway had the galley proofs back from the publisher, and it was in Sun Valley that he pored over those galleys, looking for spots in the book he wanted to add to or delete, and doing much of his rewriting.

World War II came and Ernest Hemingway left the States to become a war correspondent. After returning in 1945, he married Mary Welsh, his fourth and final wife. The following year he returned to Idaho for what

Main Street, Ketchum

was to become a fifteen-year romance with the place, which ended only with his death in 1961.

"I can remember when Ketchum had horizontal boards for sidewalks along a couple of blocks; there were no sidewalks otherwise," Mary Hemingway recalls of her early visits to Idaho. "In the autumn we used to get out there—seldom for dove season, seldom for the first of September, but after that—and there was

Sun Valley Village Square

140

hardly anyone around."

Hemingway liked Sun Valley and Ketchum at that time of the year, when there were few people around and he could wander the hills and saunter down to the Alpine Bar to talk with friends in peace.

And Sun Valley—especially Pat Rogers, the crusty old manager—loved to have him. They made it easy for him to want to stay around. Mary Hemingway's not sure her husband would think his status as a Sun Valley resident meant that much to the resort's image. "I think he would think that was pretentious, perhaps," she said. "But he did invite other friends of his to come and stay, paying friends, natch. We got—I don't remember any of the details or finances—this sitting room with a fireplace and French windows and whatnot, and two bedrooms and two baths, at a very reduced rate during the fall. It was not an outright gift from Averell, but it was comparable to whatever they charged in the village or the other motels."

Mary Hemingway does remember, however, that when they moved out of their rooms—usually before Christmas, when the Sun Valley winter season started—"the rent jumped up to something like four hundred dollars a day, and the suite was inhabited by some of the Hollywood people." Mary is quick to point out that she and her husband were accorded such "special treatment" only a couple of years.

The Hemingways led a slow, rather idyllic life while they stayed in the lodge. Hemingway usually worked in the morning, but before he started he would always slip

Kneeling: Hemingway, Taylor Williams, Gregory Hemingway (second from r.); standing: (l.) Jack Hemingway, (r.) Patrick Hemingway

on an overcoat and find Mary some breakfast. "It was very peaceful and quiet," she said. "In those days the only restaurant open in the off season was the Ram. Ernest used to trot over to the Ram and bring me back coffee and a bun or something."

Hemingway mixed well with the local people, and in fact developed some of his closest friendships in the tiny Idaho hamlet of Ketchum. Mary and Ernest loved to visit the Alpine, one of Ketchum's landmark bars on Main Street.

"The Alpine was the principle restaurant in those days," said Mary. "They used to do a sizzling steak platter, you know, with the french fries and coleslaw and a great huge inch-and-one-half-thick sirloin or T-bone, and it was only $1.50 or $1.75. It's comic compared to the prices of today."

They would go to the Alpine to eat, to talk, and sometimes to gamble. Mary Hemingway described it as "very gay and fun," the poker games adding a frontier zest to everything.

"All the bars had a few poker games going, and our favorite place of course was the Alpine, which was run by a friend of Ernest's," said Mary. "It had a big bar with roulette and poker and of course slot machines."

The Hemingways were not chronic gamblers but, when conditions warranted staying inside, they'd usually head for the Alpine. "When we patronized it, it would mostly be on a rainy day when we couldn't go hunting," said Mary. "We'd go and gamble maybe fifteen or twenty dollars in the afternoon. That was about it. When I finished with my twenty, I went home."

Mary isn't really sure just what Ernest's limit for losing was. "I don't know what kind of stakes he gave himself; sometimes he'd come back triumphant. But he was never a serious gambler. It was not one of those compulsive things for him at all."

What was compulsive for "Papa" Hemingway at Sun Valley was hunting, which he did with Lloyd Arnold, Gary Cooper, and a number of other faithful friends.

Cooper, perhaps because he represented the ruggedness and freedom of spirit Hemingway so admired, had been one of the author's best friends since 1939. When Hemingway first visited Sun Valley, Lloyd Arnold tried to set up a hunting date for him with Cooper. Actor and author talked at length over the phone, and although Cooper's movie commitments kept him from going to

Cooper and Hemingway

143

Gable and "Coop"—a fair day's bag

Sun Valley that time, the friendship that started then lasted until 1961, the year both died.

Mary Hemingway and Rocky Cooper had as much fun as their husbands; the hunting may not have thrilled them quite so much, but they enjoyed their time together. "Cooper lived very simply, as we did," said Mary. "It was a matter of tooling down the road looking for pheasants. Or when duck season opened, we'd take picnic stuff and a bota for wine, and we'd walk around in the sagebrush all day long, bang away sometimes and come back, and the guys in the coal room in the lodge would hang our birds for us. When I shot a deer one year, they hung my deer there. We used to hang our birds there and then dine together at the Ram. It was a pretty simple life. Since we were getting up at the crack of dawn frequently, we went to bed fairly early."

Hemingway stayed close to Ketchum and Sun Valley a great deal of the time during the forties. Then in 1952 he left, and didn't return again until 1958. A wanderer, Hemingway spent much of the early fifties in Italy with Mary; then he would come back, visit Key West for a time, and then Cuba.

"We had the great luxury of never having to bracket our time," reminisced Mary Hemingway. "Like when we drove across country, for example, sometimes it used to take us ten days to drive down to Key West. That's because if we liked a place, we'd stay around for a couple of days and look at the local bars and the local museums, or we frequently ran into friends or something of that sort."

But Hemingway always yearned to return to Sun Valley and his friends—Lloyd and Tillie Arnold, guides Taylor Williams and Don Anderson, and others.

"He loved the people; he loved the mountains," Mary said. "He loved the easy informality of living. He didn't even have to put a tie on to go to the Ram at night. He loved living outdoors. We lived outdoors most of the time in Pilar; we went fishing an awful lot in Cuba, you know. And we were outdoors all the time in Africa. That's the kind of a life he loved."

Mary Hemingway, herself a noted writer used to dealing with affluent, well-bred people, was never surprised that her husband could mingle so easily with the Sun Valley locals. "They really thought of him as family— Pappy and Tillie Arnold and some of the people who worked for [Taylor] Williams," said Mary. "That was the kind of a guy he was. His best friends in Cuba were fishermen, many of them uneducated, even in Spanish I mean. And you know, some of his best friends in Cuba were bartenders."

Even though he spent a great deal of his middle and later life in Sun Valley and Ketchum, Hemingway never wrote at length about the place. He wrote constantly while there—he did a good portion of his work on *The Moveable Feast* while at Ketchum—but his thoughts then were about distant places, wars, fishing in the Caribbean, and other tales that didn't involve Ketchum, Sun Valley, or Idaho.

"You know, Bill Janss wanted me to dig up stuff that Ernest had written about that part of the country," said

Duck hunting, Silver Creek

Mary Hemingway. "The only thing we found was a thing which was published in one of the sports magazines [*True*, 1951]. It was called "The Shot" and it's supposed to be fiction, but it is a true story about how they went hunting mountain sheep up the Pahsimeroi. He and Taylor Williams and at least one of his sons. By chance, after having huffed and puffed up

A proud father-and-son team: Papa and Patrick

this mountain, this guy happened to shoot two mountain sheep instead of one. There were two of them and he didn't realize it. That's the only piece he did based in that area."

Mary Hemingway doesn't know why her husband didn't write about Idaho; she can only guess. "There were lots of things he could have written about, and he was happy with the place," she said. "There isn't a reason, really. I guess nobody asked him for a piece about it, is all."

Of Hemingway's three sons—Gregg, Patrick, and Jack—it was Jack who would be most influenced by Sun Valley. Gregg became a New York City doctor and Patrick went on to Africa to work in animal conservation. Jack spent time in the army and then became a San Francisco stockbroker, but in 1967 he returned to Ketchum to live full-time with his wife Puck, an Idaho native, and three daughters—Mariel; Muffet, author of the best-selling novel *Rosebud;* and Margaux, internationally famous model and movie star.

Jack's memory of what it was like when he first visited Sun Valley with his father in 1940 hasn't dimmed. "It was the place where I first discovered charging—that's really fantastic," Hemingway laughed. "You know, you could sign your name for something; you didn't have to have the money. It was sort of a sinister thing. My father said it was one of the worst things that ever happened, us kids discovering about signing your name."

To a young man, Sun Valley was a strong experience.

Mary Hemingway

"The star system was in full force then, you know, and these people were really like gods. You'd see them and your mouth dropped down. They had a trio of gals from Salt Lake City in the dining room that were absolutely gorgeous, and they sang at all meals except breakfast. They'd come around to the tables and it sent shivers up my spine, seeing those beautiful girls singing right at you 'I'll Never Smile Again.'"

Jack visited again in August of 1941 and stayed until December. Then he was scheduled to leave for Wake Island, where his father had arranged a job for him with Morrison-Knudson, a giant construction company based in Boise. But Jack Hemingway never made it to Wake, because on December 7, the Japanese bombed Pearl Harbor and the war was on.

"I left here December fifth and went back to Chicago December seventh," said Hemingway. "I was going to get my clothes together, say goodbye to Mom and things. I was going to work a year at Wake before going to college."

College had to wait until 1946. Jack Hemingway joined the army, served his time, and then, after visiting his father in Cuba for six weeks, went back to Sun Valley to become a bellhop in the lodge. Suddenly he found himself carrying the bags of people he used to know socially through his father. And he found out about tipping.

"You found out who—well, you had 'dimers' and you had sort of decent people," Hemingway explained. "I had a little bit of a problem. I knew a lot of the people who were the big tippers, and it was as embarrassing for them as it was for me. So I had the kind of deal where I took the 'run-of-the-mill' guys and the other fellows would take the guys who were potential big-tippers. Oftentimes they weren't."

Jack worked for Pat Rogers, "a very, very nice guy, but also a nervous wreck," said Hemingway. "The one thing that stands out to me most strongly in remembering Pat is just before the season opening, December fifteenth or seventeenth or whenever it would be. They'd be just nervous as hell about whether they had enough snow or not. I remember the first winter after the war, in 1946, they were just sweating it out, and Pat would break out. His face was a little bit ruddy anyway, but he'd break out in absolutely bright things of hives. He was a nervous wreck."

Jack Hemingway was eventually promoted from bellboy to desk clerk, a move which caused him immediate financial worries. "I got promoted to desk, whereby my salary rose from fifty to a hundred and twenty-five dollars [a month]," said Hemingway. "But then all of a sudden I didn't have any tips. My income dropped from about four hundred dollars down to a hundred and twenty-five. I was making less money, but I was a young man on the way up!" he laughed.

Jack Hemingway skied a great deal at Sun Valley before leaving for Montana State University in Bozeman for a brief fling at college. Although it's said his father never skied—at least he was never spotted on the slopes at Dollar Mountain or Baldy—Jack says Hemingway *was* a skier. "He was one of the early skiers, but not here. He skied some, quite a lot when I was a little kid in Austria. But at this area here, I don't think he ever skied. He had a bum knee from World War I, and I think the thing got very stiff on him. I think he could have done it if he'd wanted to, but I think he just preferred other things."

Jack Hemingway and his family are very much a part of the Sun Valley area, and Mary Hemingway returns every July to the Ketchum home she and Ernest lived in during the last years of his life. She stays through October, the time of year she considers the most beautiful in the Wood River Valley. "You can watch the aspens turn color, and there's a stream below the house, and once in a while, every year, we see a few deer come down. And there's the birds, all different kinds of birds. We always get a few doves in the fall." Mary laughed and added, "But we wouldn't dream, of course, of shooting the doves on our own place. We'd go twenty or thirty miles down the road to look for somebody else's doves!"

When Ernest Hemingway left the Sun Valley area in 1949, he was even then feeling pressed by the number of people coming there after the war. "I think one reason we decided to go to Italy was that he thought he was getting kind of crowded out west," Mary recalled.

Still, Hemingway returned to Idaho in 1958, in spite of the newly crowded conditions of Sun Valley, ready to resume his life of bird shooting with his cronies. He spent most of his time in Ketchum, cavorting with

Jack Hemingway, 1941

River Run lift

Lloyd and Tillie Arnold and the rest of the Sun Valley crowd. But Ernest Hemingway was deteriorating physically. Much of his drive seemed gone, and his friends, notably Lloyd Arnold, recognized this. In 1961 Hemingway flew to the Mayo Clinic to see if there was a medical reason for his condition. He came back, apparently on the way to recovery. But it was only temporary.

On May 13, 1961, Gary Cooper died in Los Angeles of cancer. On July 2, 1961, Ernest Hemingway died of a self-inflicted gunshot wound at his Ketchum home. The world press screamed the news that America's greatest author, the man who lived the things he wrote and seemed to have done everything a man could ever want to do, was dead. And the world mourned.

Hemingway, Jane Russell in the field

Rocky Cooper with Ernest, Mary, and "Coop"

Ernest Hemingway was buried in a private ceremony in Ketchum's quaint little cemetery, while magazine and newspaper photographers clicked their cameras from outside its boundaries. A nationful of people wanted to be at the graveside, but just fifty were invited.

Johnny Lister was one of them. "It was by invitation only," recalled Lister. "The press was kept outside the fence and there were just the fifty around the grave. Standing next to me and my wife was the local taxi driver."

The manager of Sun Valley was not there. By 1961, this was no longer Pat Rogers but a man named Winston McCrea, whom Papa hadn't cared for, and so he was not invited, according to Lister. "Mary loved to say Papa had a three-hundred-and-sixty-degree bullshit detector, and the one thing he could not stand was a phony. You had to be real, you had to be open, you had to be honest. You had to call things like they were, and if you didn't you didn't last. I don't think Papa created that in Sun Valley, but I think Papa fit into Sun Valley because it was that same kind of thing.

"After Papa killed himself, the town of Ketchum absolutely coalesced around Mary," Lister said. "They wouldn't tell—for instance, the taxi drivers wouldn't tell—where the Hemingway house was. The people in the town would not tell. The publicity-seeker and the person after celebrities never had an easy time at Sun Valley. Never."

The days of Ernest Hemingway are gone forever in the Wood River Valley. The open places he loved have been snapped up by developers for condominiums, year-round homes, and commercial developments, and the people stream into Sun Valley in endless droves.

But the memories linger, with his friends, his sons, and Mary Hemingway. One day, after having those memories kicked loose in conversation with Maria Cooper Janis, daughter of Gary Cooper and wife of concert pianist Byron Janis, Mary Hemingway reminisced about what those early days in Sun Valley meant to her.

"Maria was saying it was a time in her life that was very important to her, but I think that's what it meant for all of us," said Mary. "It was a time of, you know, good cheer and easy living. I don't mean easy living from the standpoint of not going full-out in whatever

"Papa"

endeavor. If we were going pheasant hunting we were serious about that, and used to practice a lot with the skeet and shooting trap and all that sort of thing. God knows I hunted seriously one year, up and down mountains, all over the place, looking for a buck. There must have been eight different mornings, getting up in the cold black, four or five in the morning, going down and

Hemingway Memorial

having breakfast at the Alpine, and then heading for the mountains and getting out of the car just at daybreak, and then climbing those mountains. And it was cold, really cold, and I finally got one in my sights and whammo! And we hung him in the room at the lodge. It was a time of—well, there were not many introverts; at least if there were we didn't run into them. This was all a pretty extroverted, happy-go-lucky place. People were doing what they liked to do."

There has been some contention that maybe Sun Valley, and Idaho, wasn't Hemingway's favorite place after all, that somewhere else—Montana, Cuba, or perhaps Africa—was his ideal.

Jack Hemingway's not sure what his father would have said; he can only guess. "If somebody were to say 'where's your favorite place?,' I think I would probably pick some river, and I wouldn't care what state it was in. You know, it's what the place has for you. He didn't do bird shooting in Montana, except for pistol shooting for grouse in the fall, and that was the thing he loved to do the best. But this area, going down to Gooding [Idaho], south of Carey and Richfield and that area around there, I'd have to say that he really liked this better. If he'd liked someplace else better, he would have lived there."

They buried Ernest Hemingway in Idaho soil, in the shadow of Baldy, the great mountain which dominates Sun Valley and the lives of all who pass through it. From its peak, 3,400 feet above the Wood River Valley, you can scan the country he loved. It was only fitting that a memorial be erected to Hemingway on the road to Trail Creek Cabin, where he laughed and drank at numerous parties.

The words of his love for that country are carved in granite there. They are taken from the eulogy Hemingway delivered at the funeral of his close friend Gene Van Guilder, who died from a gunshot wound on a hunting trip in 1939. The Hemingway Memorial tells the story of Ernest Hemingway and Idaho adequately enough:

Best of All he Loved the Fall
The Leaves Yellow on the Cottonwoods
Leaves Floating in the Trout Streams
And Above the Hills
The High Blue Windless Skies
. . . Now he Will Be a Part of Them Forever.

Sun Valley arrival

While Sun Valley was to grow in size and in legend as the years passed, it was undoubtedly in its glory during the pre-war years from 1937 to 1941. As the country pulled out of the depression and Hitler squawked maniacally from Germany, America gaped at pictures of the cream of society playing at the Queen of Resorts.

Actors flocked to the area, and it was only natural that Hollywood would find it a good place to shoot films. And what could be better for the stars than to be on location at a place where, after a rugged day's shooting, they could return to the luxury they were so used to?

After Claudette Colbert shot the opening scenes to "I Met Him in Paris," Spencer Tracy followed up by shooting the opening scenes to his African odyssey, "Stanley and Livingstone," in the Boulder Mountains, ten miles outside Sun Valley. And of course much of "Sun Valley Serenade," starring Sonja Henie, was filmed at the resort.

Sonja Henie may have been the world's classiest ice skater, but she wasn't much on skis. In fact, she had to have a stand-in for the skiing sequences (and even sent one in for some of the skating scenes, according to Tillie Arnold). Gretchen Fraser, pigtailed and fresh out of high school, substituted for Henie "any time she skied." Henie would be photographed in the studio, with the wind blowing her hair and scenery flashing by.

Gretch Fraser also stood in for Margaret Sullivan when "The Immortal Storm" was filmed in Sun Valley. "It was kind of a spy story and they ended up leav-

A Flower in Every Room

. . . Pappy Rogers' Reign

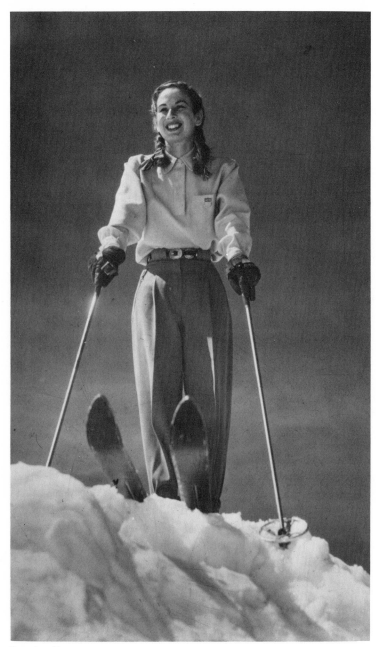

Gretchen Fraser

ing at night and escaping from Germany,'' said Gretch. "All I remember was she skied in a skirt, and this was ridiculous. With socks to here—and it'd be ten below. I'd make one run and the whole back of that skirt would be filled with snow. You got flesh-colored tights and you'd have frostbite in two minutes. And my bangs stood up, so they'd have to glue them down to make them stay.''

Much later, in the 1950's, "Bus Stop" was filmed just outside Sun Valley, and the cast—including Marilyn Monroe—stayed at the resort.

For all its rustic charm and elegant beauty, the uniqueness of Sun Valley had to be worked at constantly. A guest arriving at the Shoshone railroad station could not be expected to hop on the commuter bus to Ketchum and step off, pick up the key, and check into his room. That could happen in any hotel from Los Angeles to Boston. A few guests, like Gary Cooper, didn't demand or even want anything out of the ordinary. But most guests expected something different, and the Sun Valley management usually delivered it.

The manager is important to any hotel, but in a resort like Sun Valley, which gains or loses its reputation largely through the stories that are told by guests after they leave, a good manager is absolutely essential; he must be able to manufacture goodwill.

The man who stands above all other managers in Sun Valley's forty-year history is Pat "Pappy" Rogers, who ran the area from 1938 to 1952. Sun Valley had trouble finding a manager satisfactory to Averell Harriman, until Rogers joined the staff in August of 1938. One of the problems seemed to be the early managers' limited experience within the railroad company itself.

"We tried to get someone from the outside to run it, but we found out it didn't work," said Harriman. "And so I got Mr. Rogers, who was running the North Rim Lodge and camping areas for the Union Pacific at the Grand Canyon. He had a lot to do with the railroad and had the knack for giving first-rate service."

Pat Rogers was a big, hearty man who loved baseball, loved to work, and above all, loved to have people leave Sun Valley with good news about the service they'd received.

At one time, Rogers had been a professional baseball player, and the only thing that could distract him from his duties as manager was summer softball. Rogers would organize teams and then form a league, and during summer evenings in the soft, cool shadow of Baldy, would lead his team against its opponents with a vengeance.

Louie Stur, who managed Sun Valley Lodge for a short period during the sixties, was a young Sun Valley employee when Rogers was manager. Although Stur wasn't an avid softball fan he went and watched because it was expected of him. "I used to enjoy going out there just to see the emotional development. He was really crazy about the whole thing. I knew very well that if somebody didn't show up out on the diamond he would just raise all kinds of hell."

One day during the summer Rogers had scheduled a

Sonja Henie, Don Fraser congratulate Gretchen on Olympic showing

game and was stalking through the lodge in his sweatshirt, carrying his softball glove, when he came upon the assistant manager. The unfortunate man was still dressed in his work clothes, and Rogers stormed up to him. Stur still remembers the exchange between the two. "It went something like this:

"Rogers: 'Why aren't you out on the softball field?'

Sun Valley softball

"Assistant manager: 'Well, I am sorry Mr. Rogers, but I am busy with some guests.'

"Rogers: 'The hell with it, you get out here and play!'

"The assistant manager played."

But if Rogers was like a restless lion before the game, he was like an enraged bull during it.

"People liked to heckle him because he responded so well, and at times violently," said Stur. "So here he was, an outfielder, and people kept making remarks, and he got redder and redder in the face and angrier and angrier. Finally, he ran in to the grandstands and he looked up and said, 'You, you up there, you are fired.'

"So this person looked down at the red-faced man glaring up at him and said, 'Mr. Rogers, I am sorry, but you can't fire me. I am not an employee. I am a guest.'"

That didn't stop Rogers.

"Well, then get the hell out of the valley," Rogers shouted back at the person.

"You know, everybody knew what a gold-hearted, marvelous gentleman he was, so you know everybody laughed," said Stur. "Eventually he sent this person flowers and drinks and it was all taken care of, but it wasn't an episode that we all talked about often. I found out later it was Clara Spiegel of Ketchum who was heckling Pat Rogers. She knew he could not stand it."

Rogers was in the habit of firing employees on the spot at softball games if they made a serious mistake. One day, a young college student working in Sun Valley for the summer made a particularly costly blunder, and Rogers bellowed, "You're fired!" The young man, his head on his chest, walked off the field. The next day Rogers was in Ketchum and noticed the young man standing at the bus stop with his suitcase at his feet. Rogers walked over and asked him what he was doing there.

"You fired me last night. Don't you remember?" the student said.

Rogers turned red and pointed toward Sun Valley. "Get back there and don't pay any attention to what I say from now on!"

Before Rogers hired him, Louie Stur had been in graduate school at the University of Nebraska. "I think that the nice people who arranged my scholarship thought they would do a Hungarian a favor by putting him into an environment that is like the great Hungarian plains," Stur explained. "But my hometown was right on the edge of the Alps, and all my family were skiers and mountaineers. I was a mountain boy, and I just hated Nebraska. I enjoyed very much going to

Pat Rogers

graduate school, but the first opportunity that presented itself to get back into the mountains, even for just a short time, I grabbed at it."

Stur went to Sun Valley in 1951, supposedly to drive a bus. "Pappy Rogers hired me and I received a pass on the railroad to come out to Sun Valley," said Stur. "After I arrived I dropped in to visit Mr. Rogers and tried to find out what my duties would be. Typically, Mr. Rogers was very gracious and treated me like a father or a potentate of some kind."

Somehow Rogers had found out Stur played the accordian—he might have seen it on an application for employment, or he might just have assumed that, since Stur was Hungarian, he must play the accordian. "He said, well, you just go and sign up to play in the Ram show every Thursday night. I said, well, that is fine Mr. Rogers, but what will my hotel duties be? He said don't worry about your hotel duties. You just go play your accordian at the Ram."

So Stur played his accordian on Thursday evenings and, instead of driving a bus, he was assigned to the lodge as its night accountant. It was there he began to see the crispness and thoroughness in Pappy Rogers.

When he first began his night job, Stur's immediate superiors told him they didn't care what he did with his time, until the clock struck 5:45 in the morning. "At that time, Mr. Rogers would walk through the lobby every day without fail, and I was to stand at attention and say, 'Good morning, Mr. Rogers; how are you today?'" said Stur. "And sure enough, every day that happened every time. You see, he would get up and see the five a.m. streamliner people off. We had a bus that left at five and went to Shoshone. Mr. Rogers was up every morning and walked through the entire facility, and he always used the same route. So he always arrived at the same place at the same time."

After attending to his morning duties, Rogers would ride the lift to the Roundhouse, which sits at the top of lower Baldy and overlooks Sun Valley and Ketchum. There he would help serve lunch.

"That was the only restaurant on the mountain, so everybody walked through, and he had a nice chat with everyone as he ladled out the soup," Stur explained.

Pappy Rogers tried to be a little bit of everything—grouch, friend, boss, brother—and it usually worked. Johnny Lister, who was Sun Valley's music director for twenty years, recalls the time General George Marshall was visiting Sun Valley.

"He was under tight security," said Lister. "I was playing for a cocktail party in the Redwood Room and very often, because I was the one focal point in the room other than the bar, people would be concentrated around the piano."

Marshall was talking to Rogers, bemoaning the fact that although he loved Sun Valley, he couldn't get free of the constraints of being General George Marshall. Rogers replied that Sun Valley was different; that he could walk freely there and not even be recognized. Rogers promised to send a car by next day, and the driver would show Marshall where he could go without

Edgar Bergen and (chilly) Charlie McCarthy

Spencer Tracy

John Wayne

163

being bothered.

"The next night there was another cocktail party," said Lister, "and once again Mr. Rogers and General Marshall were standing beside the piano. Marshall was absolutely radiant; he was just glowing with his report of his day. He said, 'I have had the most glorious day! You're absolutely right; I've never seen a place like this before in my life. I could be absolutely free, I could go wherever I wanted. People looked at me, but I didn't feel at all the same as I do in the city.'"

Pat Rogers had added another name to the list of important people who left Sun Valley feeling fulfilled.

To Louie Stur, the way Pat Rogers conducted himself around the hotel was the way any hotel manager should have approached the job. "He was a real hotelman in the old sense of the word, and I say this because perhaps this would express somewhat that he didn't care much about profit-and-loss statements or money. He would just give away the whole place, and of course he was loved by everyone, guests and employees; he was just very generous and very understanding. He loved people, and this was his life. Rather than sitting back in an office somewhere and working on records and finances and this type of thing."

But then, Stur said, "of course we lost our shirts while under his reign, which I am sure no business organization would tolerate too long. So when people talk about the good old times, it is an historical thing. I am always realistic and I say, well, there is no way that an organization could go on that way year after year,

Leonard Bernstein

Playing in the Ram

losing that kind of money, and have somebody up there liking it. Sure, it is nice for everybody who is here, but something has to be done about it."

Something was done about it, of course. "Somebody up there," specifically the Union Pacific hierarchy, didn't like the way Rogers threw money around, gave out free rooms, and in general ran Sun Valley as if it was his own private inn.

By 1952, Averell Harriman had been away from actual control of Union Pacific and Sun Valley for almost eleven years. The war had taken him first to London to administer the lend-lease program there, and then to Russia as America's ambassador. Then he became Secretary of Commerce and severed all his business connections with Sun Valley.

"I couldn't have taken an active interest in it," said Harriman. "I kept my house there, my family went there and skied, but I took no part in the management. I've had no connections with any business activity since then, except as a limited partner in my banking firm."

Without Harriman's steady hand and active participation, Union Pacific's interest in Sun Valley as a model playground for the rich waned, and they started to watch the money-flow more closely. Harriman had built Sun Valley in a pathfinder sense, wanting to stake out a skiing empire in America which would rival Europe's greatest. And as long as he maintained an active interest in it, the resort never suffered financially. One rumor was that before World War II, the Union Pacific didn't care what Sun Valley lost as long as it wasn't "more than a million dollars a year."

That may have been the case before World War II, but by 1952 the drain was beginning to be felt in Omaha. What the Union Pacific officials saw was a ski resort where rooms were given away to special guests, dinner tabs were picked up, and the company suffered as a result.

"You know, a lot of complimentary rooms and a lot of gifts of every kind is a nice thing in a hotel that runs 365 days a year and has good occupancy," said Louie Stur. "You show a good credit picture and then you give away a lot. But if you start out with a losing operation and then start giving everything away, that is a bad thing."

Though Pappy Rogers was beloved by guest and employee alike, he was nonetheless unquestionably the center of the giveaway program. In 1952, Rogers, who had played host to the stars, resigned to take a job in the Utah Parks System.

Stur isn't sure if Rogers' resignation was forced, but there's a hint it might have been. "The feeling in Union Pacific," Stur said, "was one that came to read 'We just have to change our policies somewhat within Sun Valley to put it on a more businesslike basis.'"

Ironically, Rogers' successors, however hard they tried, could never make the resort a paying proposition while it was owned by Union Pacific. Pat's departure marked the end of an era. Louie Stur is not alone in remembering Sun Valley as a reflection of Pappy Rogers, a big bear of a man who brought the resort a profit that couldn't be tallied in dollars and cents.

High above Sun Valley

166

By 1942, Sun Valley had joined such other nonessentials as nylon stockings and T-bone steaks on the luxury list for the American citizen. The nation was well into World War II and suddenly the resort no longer seemed so important.

Averell Harriman left America to head the lend-lease program in London, and William Jeffers took control of Union Pacific. Not too much later, Sun Valley was closed as a ski resort and its facilities converted to a naval hospital.

"I offered to do it," said Harriman about the decision to change Sun Valley from a playground to a hospital. "We'd have had to close it down anyway. It was the right thing to do, and it wouldn't have been possible to run this resort as a resort during the war."

Turning Sun Valley over to the Navy was indeed the patriotic thing to do for the country but, as it turned out, not necessarily for the soldiers who were sent there.

Soldiers returning from war naturally expect to have a little wine, women and song. The young navy patients could find the wine; it flowed freely in Ketchum's wide-open bars. And they could undoubtedly have a song. But the Navy decreed that for rehabilitation they needed skiing, not women.

"They were told by some psycho captain that they should ski at certain times," recalled Johnny Lister, who was a chaplain's assistant at Sun Valley during that period. "The end result was that they would go downtown and get drunk and then get thrown in the jug. Well, the whole thing was miserable, and even the

Union Pacific Bows Out

. . . the New Host

Ann Sothern

hard-to-convince Navy gradually changed the focus."

One of the problems was that the men figured if they were healthy enough to go skiing on Dollar or Baldy, the Navy would consider them fit for battle and ship them back to the South Pacific. As a result, many kept a low profile and feigned sickness to keep off the mountain and, by their reasoning, out of the war.

World War II ended in September, 1945, and in 1946 Sun Valley reopened, ready to resume its role as the queen of the world's ski resorts. And it did, but with changes. Instead of aiming primarily at the rich and famous, Sun Valley began broadening its appeal to get other people to come in and enjoy the unique climate and facilities.

The crowds returned, and in greater numbers. Of course, along with the growing throngs of new guests, there were still the rich and famous. Ann Sothern, one of television's early comediennes, and star of the series "Private Secretary" and "The Ann Sothern Show," became one of Sun Valley's most faithful visitors, and later a resident.

"There used to be a group that would come, like the Gary Coopers and Merle Oberon, the Van Johnsons, June Allyson, the [Darryl] Zanucks and Claudette Colbert," said Sothern. "We were all friends, you see, so we all made it a sort of meeting place for the holidays."

Sothern became a regular wintertime guest, skiing Baldy with great gusto. She also became famous for the weekly poker game she hosted, which included a few ski instructors, the mayor, and a real estate agent or two.

There were other parties the forties-and-fifties crowd used to throw, and they were usually held at one or another rustic building just outside Sun Valley, often reached by horse-drawn sleighs.

"If we wanted to give a great party, I'd take over Trail Creek Cabin or Dollar Cabin," said Sothern. On New Year's eve, the Hollywood crowd, with a few locals mixed in, would gather at Trail Creek, drink late, and play games like pin-the-tail-on-the-donkey. There were always surprises for the unsuspecting who thought they were really playing pin-the-tail. Sothern explained: "You were blindfolded, so when you reached to put the tail on the donkey you'd go right into a can of lard."

In 1957, Ann Sothern discovered a new side to the area. "In those days, I never knew Sun Valley except in winter," she said. "I had never gone there in the summertime, I think, until 1957; I fell in love with it, was enchanted with it, and bought a little house there in 1958." She lived in that house until 1968.

Sun Valley left different impressions on different people. When Fernando Lamas arrived to film a segment of the "I Love Lucy" series with Lucille Ball and Desi Arnaz, he was asked by somebody, "Oh, Fernando, don't you just love Sun Valley?"

Lamas's reply was, "Well, it's all right if you like white."

The abundance of white drew a new class of skiers to Sun Valley—the ski bums. They worked for low wages but didn't seem to care, because Sun Valley would give them a ski pass and that's all they really wanted. Some

Lowell Thomas

169

MGM film crews setting up

Louis Armstrong, rarin' to go

of the early ski bums did quite well. Warren Miller, who camped out in a trailer at the bottom of Baldy all winter after the resort reopened in 1946, stayed on and became one of the country's best-known makers of ski films. Ed Scott started his own ski pole factory, later expanded it into boots, and parlayed the business into the well-known Scott Company.

But most of those who came to fly down Sun Valley's deep powder and work at menial jobs didn't strike it rich. They would work a season or two and move on, drifting back to college or into marriage. If a person stayed more than two or three years, it generally meant he was hooked on Sun Valley and might end up staying the rest of his life in the village.

There seemed to be something about Sun Valley, from its start, that rendered the social caste system inoperable. In the beginning, employees and guests mixed freely. Jack Hemingway remembers it that way.

"There was a great sense of informality; there were no rules against mixing with the guests," said Hemingway. That was prior to World War II. After the war Union Pacific tried to impose a sort of class structure by ordering the employees not to fraternize with the guests. It didn't last long, and soon the help were once again mingling with the high and mighty.

To Johnny Lister, it was a special time and feeling. "It was the closest thing to a classless society I have ever seen," said Lister. "It was enormously egalitarian and very naturally so. It was not something put on; it was not something phony. I feel there's still a great deal

of that there. It was a place where you could be skiing with somebody who was a dishwasher and find out he had a doctorate from MIT. Typical is Scotty [Ed Scott], who came out to Sun Valley as a ski bum. Well, he was one among so many beautifully educated people. He had to get his act together and find something that he could do in the area, which worked out very nicely for him. For many others it was like a therapy. It was a place away from the world to sort of get yourself together again, and I watched it do that for person after person."

While Sun Valley seemed to project an image of elitism, especially during its first twenty-five years, Lister maintains that any apparent snobbishness stopped at the Shoshone train station. The real thing was not nearly as stuffy as it sometimes sounded. "That was one of the remarkable things about early Sun Valley," recalled Lister. "When you went to a city at that time, whenever you went into even a modest restaurant, you had to have a coat on and you had to have a tie. I mean that was just accepted; you weren't allowed in if you didn't. One of the amazing things about Sun Valley was the fact that I have literally seen people in blue jeans— and this even years ago—on the same floor with people in formals. The same great openness that I talked about the place having was reflected in the dress. Now it's true that there were the people who were basically more formal and consequently often they would want to dress formally. But the person who had not been involved with that formality was accepted with open arms."

Fernando Lamas, Lucille Ball

There were exceptions, of course, like the Duchin Room, the class spot at Sun Valley. The Ram and the Boiler Room, a discotheque actually located in the lodge's boiler room, were more informal.

The Duchin Room was a special place, as most of the world learned—or thought they learned—in the film "Sun Valley Serenade." Actually, the room in the movie wasn't the real thing. The filmmakers didn't feel the real thing had quite the right effect, so they built a model. But Hollywood notwithstanding, the Duchin

Room was—and still is—very special. The pianist's wife did the interior design, and Eddy Duchin was scheduled to play at its opening. But Mrs. Duchin died giving birth to their son Peter, and Duchin never performed in the room which bears his name.

The Shah of Iran was probably Sun Valley's most lavish visitor. Having seen the movie "Sun Valley Serenade," the Shah brought his queen, Soroya, to Sun Valley because he couldn't believe there was a place in the world like the small Idaho village he saw on film.

The Shah picked the fifties to visit the resort. He partied long and hard while at Sun Valley, and was entranced with the idea of taking part in a torchlight parade from the Roundhouse to the bottom of Baldy. The Shah had his way, with Sigi Engl leading the sparkling procession of skiers. And, said Sigi, "The son-of-a-gun got me to like caviar. He left me eight pounds of it that they didn't consume at one of the parties."

But while people like the Shah of Iran continued coming to Sun Valley, the resort itself was losing some of its physical charm because money for maintenance and improvements was not being poured into it as had been the case in its early years.

Union Pacific had replaced Pat Rogers with a man named Winston McCrea, who proved to be a better administrator but less of the jovial innkeeper. And McCrea was hampered by the fact that the railroad simply didn't seem to be able to spend the dollars needed to improve Sun Valley enough.

But change was on the way.

The Shah of Iran with Otto Lang

173

Bill Janss

In the late sixties, Steve McQueen visited Sun Valley and, true to the maverick style of his screen performances, immediately had a fight with a fireplace.

McQueen was staying in one of the resort's condominiums, and when it came time to light the fire, he was disgruntled to discover it was gas-fueled.

"Sometimes Steve is slightly irrational," according to Bill Janss. "He's a fine person. But he got incensed that one would have a gas fireplace with gas logs in a mountain resort, and it incensed him so that he jerked the pipes out and built a fire. Well, that was slightly dangerous, because the flue was not designed for the heat of real logs. Anyway, it worked out all right, and when Steve went away we put the artificial logs back in the fireplace."

By the time McQueen showed up at Sun Valley, it was Bill Janss, not the Union Pacific, who had to worry about such eccentricity, because he and his family and partners owned the place.

A skier from the age of six, Bill Janss had gone to college at Stanford University, where he helped form a ski team. "I really started skiing actively when I was a freshman at Stanford," he said. "And then it was every weekend in the winter."

Every weekend in the winter led to Janss's being named to the 1940 U.S. Olympic Team, only to have the thrill of his selection blunted by the fact that World War II cancelled the event. "I was very disappointed, because that would have been very exciting," Janss said. "There was a feeling about it, like you would have been going up against monsters, you know. We had seen a few of the Europeans over here, and they were always ahead of you quite a few seconds. It was because we never trained. I mean, we went skiing, but it never occurred to us to jog around a field or something.''

After the war, Janss became involved in a cattle-feeding enterprise in Arizona; but he still took numerous skiing vacations, both in Colorado and in Europe, and eventually got into the resort business. "I was involved with Aspen a great deal; I was a board member of the Design Conference and I was a trustee of the Aspen Institute for Humanistic Studies,'' said Janss, "because I had a great interest in those operations and also because I was there a great deal of the time, and could bring some input. Anyway, that's where I really developed a great amount of interest in skiing and being part of the corporation.''

Janss eventually got involved in developing the Snowmass ski area. And in 1964, when Union Pacific began to take a hard look at Sun Valley, the Janss Corporation was asked to study the facilities and make recommendations as to what could be done with the resort. What could be done, according to Janss and his partners, would require Union Pacific's shoveling five million dollars into their ailing playground.

The railroad pulled out. "When Union Pacific decided not to spend five million and preferred to sell, they looked to us to carry out the program,'' said Janss. "I think we were favored because they thought we would do a good job.''

Bill Janss

Averell Harriman knew the railroad wasn't taking proper care of Sun Valley, and so he wasn't surprised when the California Janss family agreed to purchase it for three million dollars. "Union Pacific was no longer interested in it,'' Harriman said, "and wanted someone to take it and develop it as I would have developed it if I had stayed on as chairman of the board.''

Early golfer

Janss was excited about Sun Valley, which he considered better located than Aspen in many ways. He recommended his corporation take over the resort simply because he felt its year-round potential was so great. "Colorado is very pretty and lovely, but it's not as fine as this country is for summer, because it rains every afternoon. There really aren't as many lakes and streams when you look at Colorado. Here, it's trees and lakes and streams and good snow, and we knew the advantages of being here, because we knew it had to be an all-season resort."

Janss and his partners decided to rework Sun Valley pretty thoroughly. "The place was fairly run down," said Janss, and laughed. "And I think the American architects went to Europe to see what a foreign resort looked like, and at the same time they were sending their architects to see what American resorts looked like. When their architects came over, they found every bedroom had a bath. When ours went abroad they found that, surprisingly, there was only one bathroom, in the hall. Anyway, that's the way the Challenger Inn was built. It had adjoining bathrooms and dormitories."

Conceived from a structure which appeared in "Sun Valley Serenade," the Challenger Inn had been designed as less expensive accommodations for guests— and that meant everyone couldn't have a private bath. "It was done a long time ago," said Janss, "so there's no criticism intended. They wanted the inn for people who could not afford the lodge. However, they should have said that, in ten years, if the resort is any good,

The Jansses were well known in California. Bill's father had been a pioneer developer in southern California, clearing some land near Los Angeles and building the village of Westwood, which later became the site of UCLA. In 1964, Bill and the family were partners with American Cement at Snowmass, but they decided to buy Sun Valley anyway. (Later, in 1968, they divested themselves of their Snowmass interests.)

there will be so many people here who want bathrooms we'd better have them."

Tearing out every other wall in the inn and building new bathrooms was only the beginning. "We had to just completely redo all of the rooms in the lodge and the inn. Nobody had been spending in Sun Valley for years." The five million dollar estimate the Janss Corporation had given Union Pacific turned out to be low, by the time all the bills were in. "We've put in a lot more," said Janss. "But it turns out that was a commitment that had to be made, and we kept it."

For the first thirty years of its existence, Sun Valley had been primarily a winter resort. "There was really nothing here in summer except nice old people who would sit and watch the skaters on the rink," Janss explained. "They had three asphalt tennis courts, which is like not having a court at all."

One of the first things Janss did was to build eight new tennis courts and an Olympic-size swimming pool, and then a shopping mall for the area connecting the lodge and the inn. "For that we have to give a lot of thanks to Union Pacific for planning. They separated the two," said Janss. "It gave us the perfect opportunity to create the street.

"All that year it was hell around here," Janss continued. "It was build, build, build. It was noisy and dusty. We were also able to build the Lodge Apartments, which I think are beautiful."

By the summer of 1965, Sun Valley was beginning to fill out, and in 1966 Janss led a quiet fight to have the Idaho legislature pass a bill which allowed the sale of condominiums in the state. "California had it, but there was nothing in Idaho," said Janss. "We just asked our lawyer to get it into the legislature. It was an obvious need. No one had thought about it before. It allowed us then to build a hundred and twenty-eight very small studio apartments ["ateliers"], with some two-bedroom units added on. It was my concept, and they sold out before we could finish them."

Condominiums have since grown steadily on the Valley's land. The first studio apartments were followed by Villagers I and II. The condominiums, which now range in size from studio to four-bedroom units, are purchased almost as rapidly as they are built. The newest—bigger, better, and of course more expensive than the others—boast tremendous luxury combined with tennis courts at the doorstep and unparalleled views of Baldy. All of Sun Valley's "condos" are run by Sun Valley Property Management, headed by Louie Stur. They are available for rent when their owners are not using them, and give the resort more room for more guests; there are now approximately 8,000 beds in Sun Valley, compared to about 800 when Janss took over.

On the other hand, there are those who feel that there's too much building going on in the area, attracted by Sun Valley's success. Construction projects in Ketchum, Elkhorn (a development near Sun Valley but not a part of it), and even Hailey, thirteen miles down the highway, are consuming more and more of the land. Some of the people who have been coming to

Sun Valley for years don't want to see any more growth. They have heard too much about other resort areas where "outside developers" have built too much too fast, and they worry that rapid growth will detract from the natural beauty of Sun Valley's setting.

But Sun Valley is still relatively small in the development department, and clings to its own special sort of grandeur even as it grows. Most of the developers, and certainly Bill Janss, feel that controlled growth is the answer, and numerous plans in the works seem dedicated to this concept.

"You see, we never went the route of Aspen or Vail, selling off pieces of land to developers," Janss explained. "We have pretty well controlled our own growth. In a few cases we have sold off a piece of land here and there, to people who had to build to our architectural standards. But when you look at the number of units we've added here in eleven years—we only build about sixty or seventy units a year, and that's not fast growth. It's more the normal growth you'd run into in a little Austrian town; as a matter of fact, it's slower growth than in an alpine village. I was always afraid of making mistakes and creating problems. If you grow slowly, you see your needs and you build for those needs."

Janss's concept is to develop Sun Valley along the lines of a Swiss village, which is very much the idea Union Pacific started with—although of course there are many more people, restaurants, tennis courts, ski lifts, and cultural events now. But, Janss pointed out,

"We are not sprawled out all over the community. We don't encourage cars. We don't have inconveniences. It's really continuing to grow in the way we originally thought and planned."

As condominium and other construction mushroomed, Janss, still intent on building up the summer trade, added onto the horseback and skeet-shooting facilities and improved the golf course. "It was in very sad shape," said Janss of the Sun Valley course. "It was narrow, and the rough was all rocks. Today it has wide fairways and trees, and the roughs are grass. It is a championship course."

The Sun Valley Center for the Arts and Humanities was started by Janss and his wife Anne, who died tragically in an avalanche in the winter of 1973. The work of the Center, a non-profit organization which has grown into an important educational and cultural institution, has been carried on by its director, Anne's close friend and now Bill's wife, Glenn Janss. As Bill put it, "Why go to New York, when the Louis Falco dancers come here? We're getting the drama and the music. Glenn's Center also runs the theater here, so we're getting the finest movies." Throughout the year, the Sun Valley Center also conducts workshops in the arts, including literature, dance, photography, ceramics and glassblowing, and hosts special seminars and conferences.

Bill Janss has expended much effort to restore or recapture some of the special ambience of early Sun Valley. In certain areas, this has meant trying to maintain the old Austrian way of doing things—in, for example,

Sun Valley condominiums

the elegant service and food offered in the dining establishments managed by Sun Valley Company itself.

Peter Schott's first impression of the United States was that the country had crummy Coca-Cola. In the winter of 1967, the young Austrian—barely twenty years old and speaking almost no English—stood in the Denver airport trying to cope with an example of Yankee ingenuity: a vending machine. "I put in a coin and all that came in the glass was syrup," Schott laughed. "I took a big swallow, and my first thought was, lousy, lousy Coca-Cola in the United States."

Schott was on his way from Kitzbühel, Austria, to Sun Valley, Idaho, at the behest of Bill Janss, who wanted him to cook at the Ram. The two had met through a mutual friend just that summer, and Janss was impressed with the young man's credentials, which included culinary school in Innsbruck and an apprenticeship as a chef in Kitzbühel. Schott arrived in Sun Valley the day before Christmas, quite a bit the worse for wear and not a little leary of what he was getting into. It had been no easy matter, getting from Austria to Idaho, particularly for someone who could hardly speak the language. "I began the trip riding the train to Luxemburg from Kitzbühel," recalled Schott, whose command of English is now quite good. "From Luxemburg I flew to Iceland, then to New York, and then from New York to Denver." By the time he got to Twin Falls, Schott had a miserable cold. He was feeling less than fortunate to be in America, as he sat sipping tea in a local cafe. Then "a huge cadillac" arrived to take him the ninety miles from Twin Falls to Sun Valley, and things started to look a little brighter.

Schott worked in the Ram the first season, returned briefly to Austria, then came back to Sun Valley to continue developing his talents in *haute cuisine*. By the fall of 1970 and the age of twenty-three, he was head chef of the Duchin Room.

During those first years in Sun Valley, something else was developing for Peter Schott—visa problems. As an alien visitor to the United States, Schott was in Sun Valley on a temporary visa, which, after several extensions and renewals, had finally expired. The chef had to get a permanent visa somehow, or leave the country. Sun Valley lawyers went to work; Sun Valley did not want to lose a culinary artist like Peter Schott.

At last Schott was told not to worry, that the permanent visa was as good as in hand. With this in mind, the Austrian decided to take some time off before the season rush and have a look at Mexico. He had a great time—until he came to the border to reenter the United States.

"We were at the Mexican border without anything," Schott explained. "The permanent visa hadn't gone through. No visa for the U.S., and no visa for Mexico, and, naturally, out of money, since it was the last day of vacation." He and a friend had fifteen dollars between them. Schott was literally a man without a country.

The border police finally let the two go to the American Embassy. They were given transit visas and made it back to Sun Valley, where they found the attorneys still

Warm Springs run

entangled in legal red tape. Schott's dilemma was also Sun Valley's, however, since the resort had already gone through quite a few head chefs; and so, after much hard work ("Carl Burke [Sun Valley attorney], he even talked to the Governor," Schott remembered.), the permanent visa finally came through.

In 1975, the Duchin Room was honored with membership in the world's oldest gourmet society, the *Chaîne des Rôtisseurs*, founded in Paris in 1248. Schott is determined to stay in the United States, and has built quite a reputation for himself and Sun Valley.

For Bill Janss, though, the most important thing in Sun Valley remains Bald Mountain. Janss wants his mountain to become a champion in its own right, and has to work hard to move toward that goal. By the time the family bought the resort, Baldy had been neglected for some time. "Skier days were declining," Janss recalled. "Let's see—about a thousand skiers a day at the most. All you had was the River Run side, River Run and the Exhibition lift. There was the old single lift that went from the Roundhouse to the top, and the double, which was not a high capacity double. And then they had the lift coming out of the bowls with a capacity of about two hundred and sixty.

"There was no Warm Springs," Janss continued. "There was just a trail that you skied down as you went home." The new owner had fallen in love with the Warm Springs side of the mountain back when he was studying the area for Union Pacific. "It was the obvious side—tremendously long runs on that side," he explained. The development of Warm Springs has made Baldy "a mountain that has the greatest variety in the country," Janss stated proudly. "It has the advantage of the big alpine slopes and the bowls, a very fine combination of all types of slopes and snow conditions."

Baldy's wooded flanks are now criss-crossed with forty-seven runs, with ample room for the 13,000 skiers an hour the twelve lifts can handle.

Grooming the slopes was another problem Janss encountered. In the old days, there was no grooming because there was no equipment to do it. "When it got icy," said Janss, "you just skied on ice." A proper job on Sun Valley's slopes required the proper equipment, and Janss went after it. "We went for the biggest models they had, and encouraged them to build them with much greater power, so they could handle our slopes. Ours are more demanding than, say, Colorado's. They are steeper, and seem to attract the best skiers, so they cut up the hills much faster. You get the moguls, which means daily grooming, especially on the steepest slopes. So we have a big investment in equipment, and today I think we are really doing the finest job in grooming."

If steep slopes caused some problems, they are nonetheless, Janss believes, the biggest attraction that Sun Valley has. "It's no effort to ski on a flat slope, and it's no challenge," he said. "I think it's great for beginners, but it's certainly no way to develop a skill or truly enjoy it. Turning on steeper slopes, the constant challenge of placing your turn—that, really, is what it's all

Sun Valley Lodge, 1976

Mashing moguls

about. Just cruising on the mountain is not using the sport to its full advantage. It's baitfishing as against flyfishing.''

The pull of Sun Valley is strong on Janss, as strong as it has been on the multitude of regular guests down through the years. Janss doesn't expect ever to leave the valley, or his high-ceilinged home, with its extraordinary collection of paintings, sculpture, and books, and its trout pond just outside the back door. "I can't imagine where we'd go,'' he said. "I really feel that this is going to be one of the finest places in the country. Here we are at Sun Valley, sitting in utmost privacy, with this view—we really don't see another house from here. We could be twenty miles out in the country, and yet we can walk to the village. I have trout in the pond, and the ducks come in in the fall. We get out of here occasionally, but when we do it's always exciting to return. We are always looking for the things we can bring back to make this a better valley.''

Averell Harriman's foresight and Felix Schaffgotsch's direction put Sun Valley at the top among American resorts, and, with Bill Janss's determination and initiative, that's where it seems destined to remain. The area is more accessible now and can accommodate many more residents and guests; and most people feel that the growth is thoughtfully planned and going in the right direction. As Mary Hemingway says, "It's getting a little crowded around here, but we still smile at the strangers!''

Acknowledgments

To acknowledge here all the people who helped us explore Sun Valley's legend is impossible. To all of them, our gratitude; and to the following, our special thanks:

Jean Terra, Anni Miller, Judy Beymer Knopp, Shannon Besoyan, Susi Gillis, Bill and Glenn Janss, Melissa Dodworth, Jeanne Cutaia, Skip and Esther Oppenheimer, Dr. and Mrs. James C. F. Chapman, Pete Lane, Kate Bonning, Ann Sothern, Gretchen and Don Fraser, Ernie Voigt, Betty Penson Ward, W. Averell Harriman, Johnny Lister, Mary Hemingway, Otto Lang, Ed Schafer and Union Pacific, *The Idaho Statesman* for the use of their files, the people at The Kitchen, who got us going in the morning, and especially Anne Chapman Oppenheimer, whose time, moral support, and insight proved invaluable.